中　医　科　普　系　列

Herpes Zoster
Help From Chinese Medicine

中　医　科　普　系　列

Herpes Zoster
Help From Chinese Medicine

Ye Xiao, M.S. TCM

Carl Stimson, L.AC

Edited by Carl Stimson & Zhang Nai-ge
Illustrated & Designed by Duanzhi Shiji Advertising Design Co., Ltd

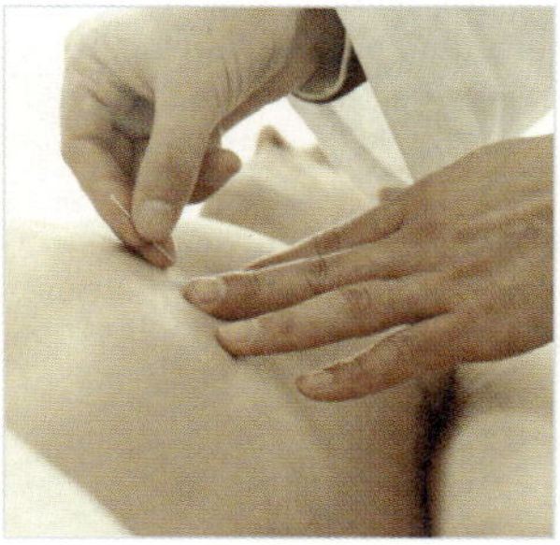

人民卫生出版社

PMPH PEOPLE'S MEDICAL PUBLISHING HOUSE

Beijing London New York

人民卫生出版社
PMPH PEOPLE'S MEDICAL PUBLISHING HOUSE
Website: http://www.pmph.com

Book Title: Herpes Zoster
Help From Chinese Medicine
中医科普系列——带状疱疹

Contact address: Bldg 3, 3 Qu, Fangqunyuan, Fangzhuang, Beijing 100078, P.R. China, phone/fax: 8610 6769 1034, E-mail: pmph@pmph.com.

For text and trade sales, as well as review copy enquiries, please contact PMPH at pmphsales@gmail.com.

Images in this book, except those belonging to PMPH and marked with Copyright © PMPH, are from the Duanzhi Shiji Advertising Company. Contact at:
Phone: 8610 6763 3273, E-mail: aijing129@163.net

First published: 2008
ISBN: 978-7-117-09749-9/R·9750

ISBN 978-7-117-09749-9

Cataloguing in Publication Data:
A catalog record for this book is available from the CIP-Database China.

Printed in The People's Republic of China

Foreword

Chinese medicine has survived in China for thousands of years, yet is still energetic and shows no sign of fading. It is wise in learning from the natural world and integrating different cultures, experienced in absorbing effective protocols and avoiding those that are not. Generous in caring not only for the health of the people of the world, but also for the balance between human beings and nature. Open-minded in the appreciation of the precise technology of biomedicine, using it to self-reflect and improve, and principled in only believing in holistic methods and protocols based on natural substances and theories. However, outstanding as Chinese medicine is, the philosophy behind it is profound and not easily understood. Because of this, the acceptance of Chinese medicine worldwide has been slow. But due to the hard work of many practitioners and their satisfied clients, Chinese medicine has been gradually recognized and accepted by people in countries around the world.

When people suffer from chronic disease they may not get good results from biomedicine. In these cases, Chinese medicine wishes to lend a hand and offer a door to health. In fact, Chinese medicine can be more effective than biomedicine in managing many diseases, and if both systems are combined the result can be particularly good.

This book focuses on managing herpes zoster with the different therapies of Chinese medicine, it is grounded in the basic theories of Chinese medicine. The aim is to offer you the chance to learn how to maintain health throughout life. To give Chinese medicine a chance is to give your health one more opportunity.

Ye Xiao
January, 2008

Guide to the Book: What Can This Book Do for Me?

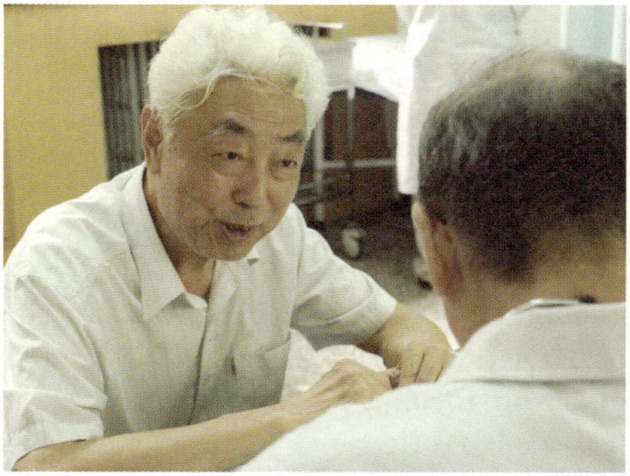

This book is designed to accomplish two things for YOU.

Explain

You may be considering getting treatment for Herpes Zoster with Chinese medicine but you have no idea what it will be like. Or you may have already begun treatment and want to know more about the theories and methods used and participate in the changes happening to you. If you find yourself in one of these situations, then this is the right book for you. This book will help you better understand what Chinese medicine is, how it can help, and what it involves. The basic theories will be introduced and the methods used by practitioners around the world will be explained in detail. Detailed explanations of techniques you may know something about, such as acupuncture and herbal medicine, as well as lesser known modalities like moxa and tui na (massage), will help clear up any questions or misconceptions as well as prepare you for visiting the clinic. And lastly, where available, excerpts from modern research and clinical trials are included to inspire confidence in the ancient theories and methods.

Guide

The second purpose of this book is to provide you with a resource that can be used to help implement lifestyle changes that will alleviate symptoms as well as increase general health and prevent future illness. There is helpful information on eating habits, exercise programs, and a variety of at-home techniques that are both easy and affordable. From experience, doctors of Chinese medicine know that with proper treatment, the amount and intensity of biomedical intervention can be reduced or even eliminated. It is our hope that with the help of this book as a guide, all kinds of medical intervention can be reduced so that your time, energy, and money can be better spent doing the things you love.

While there is a lot of valuable information in the following chapters, this book is in no way intended to substitute for the care of a trained professional. Making a proper diagnosis and prescribing effective treatments are skills that take years to master and are especially difficult in complex problems such as herpes zoster. Chinese medicine is a highly individualized system, and the help of a proper guide, especially in the beginning stages, is essential. For suggestions on how to go about finding a qualified practitioner of Chinese medicine, please see the appendix.

Table of Contents

Table of Contents

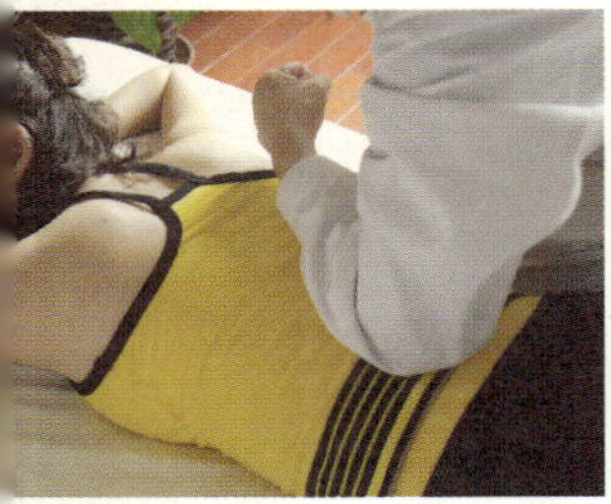

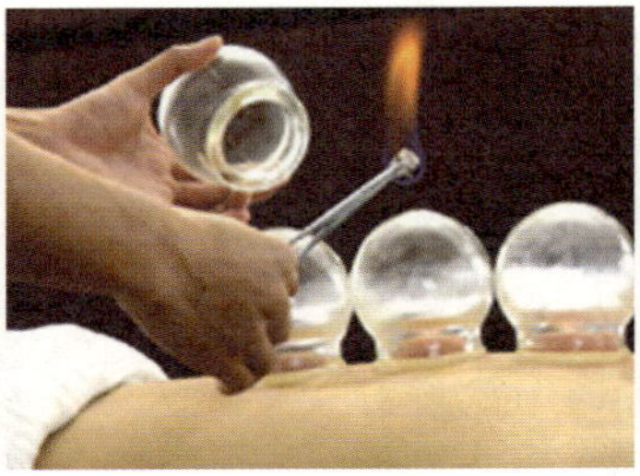
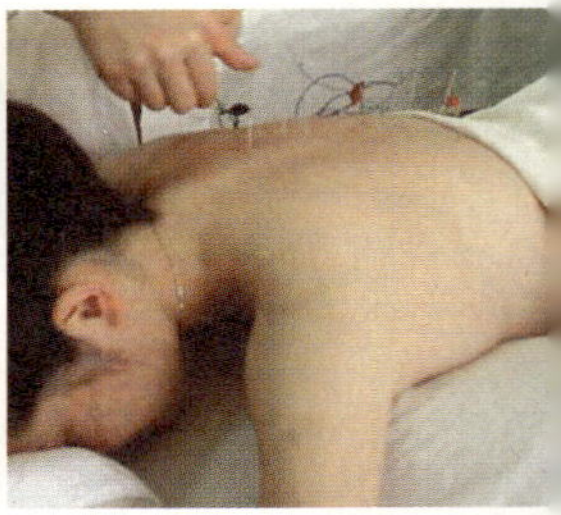

Chapter 1

Why Chinese Medicine?

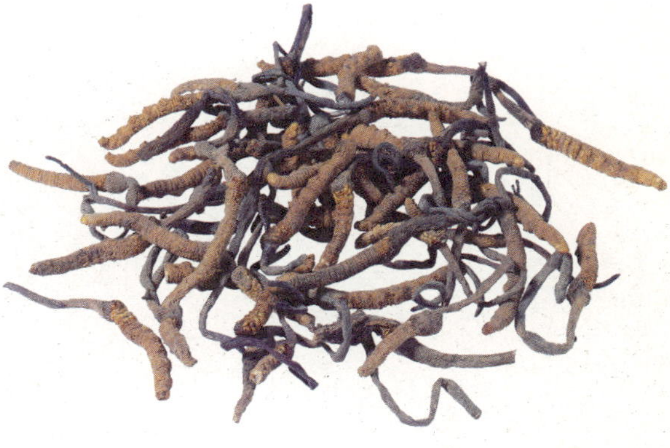

Why Chinese Medicine?

Ginseng

Chinese medicine has exploded in popularity over the past few decades. Techniques that have been used in Asia for thousands of years have finally found their way to the West and are being heartily embraced. Acupuncture, tai ji, and yin-yang theory seem to be everywhere recently. The medical community has taken notice, and US government sponsored research on Chinese medicine and other natural medicines now reaches nearly $300 million dollars every year[1]. The public is also interested and acupuncture appears in places from the Oprah Show to hip-hop lyrics.

An ancient and mysterious art, Chinese medicine has been rigorously practiced for thousands of years. There are now well established schools all over North America and Europe as well as a growing field in South America, Africa, and the Middle East, not to mention its firm establishment in all Asian countries. It is not unusual these days for hospitals in major cities to employ a practitioner of Chinese medicine and many insurance companies are choosing to cover it due to its efficacy, low cost, and safety.

As most people grew up with conventional biomedicine, it is difficult to resist comparing it to Chinese medicine. Most people outside of Asia still do not consider Chinese medicine a scientific medical practice. There is no shortage of critics and doubters in the biomedical community, but most of these critics have had no significant training in Chinese medicine and are largely ignorant of its theories and techniques.

Despite the temptation and tendency to, Chinese medicine can not be compared across the board with modern biomedicine. To quote Judith Farquhar from her lecture in Beijing 2005, "The comparison should engage with realities more than with ideals." Before comparisons are made, those making comparisons should be familiar with each system. While evaluation of the efficacy of Chinese medicine needs to be in line with modern research standards, the unique characteristics of diagnosis and the modalities used in Chinese medicine make it difficult to fit it into research methods that have been tailored for biomedical study. Furthermore, there are fundamental differences between Chinese medicine and biomedicine that lie outside the realm of lab tests and clinical trials. The two systems are different in terms of their philosophy, principles, and approaches to treatment. As you read this book, we hope you will begin to understand the power and subtlety the Chinese system has to offer.

Chinese medicine can offer a transformational experience for those who suffer from herpes zoster or any other disease. It is more than relieving pain. It is about recovering your natural ability to heal. Chinese medicine can help relieve discomforts which may not go away even if the pain from the herpes zoster goes away. The ultimate goal is to improve your quality of life, maximize your sense of well-being, eliminate or delay complications, and achieve a longer and happier life.

Pulse Examination

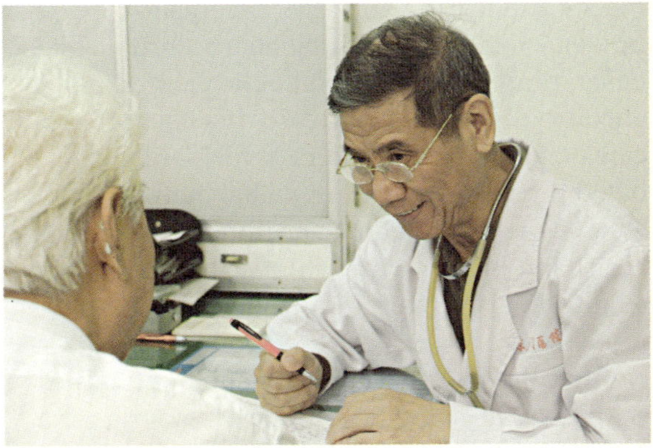

Zhou Ping-an, Professor at Beijing University of Chinese Medicine

Astragalus

While biomedicine thrives in emergency rooms and during surgery, it seems to lose its power when faced with the many chronic diseases plaguing modern society, especially chronic diseases like heart disease, stroke, cancer, and lung disorders, which are now labeled the world's leading killers by the WHO. What's more, many medications used in biomedicine have formidable side effects. For example, acyclovir, an antiviral drug, effectively restrains viral DNA duplication and is commonly used in the management of herpes zoster. At the same time, it may also trigger a series of side-effects, including a drug induced rash, perspiration, hypotension, nausea, headache, abdominal pain, mental difficulties, and decreased white blood cells.

Administering pharmaceuticals that substitute for a weakened bodily function or artificially replace an insufficient substance can make a patient's laboratory results look better and may even help the patient feel better, but often come with uncomfortable side-effects and lead to difficult complications over time. Therapies such as these are clearly not aimed at restoring the body's own ability to maintain health.

This is not meant to say that biomedicine does not have its merits. Many drugs produced by modern science do wonderful things with very few side-effects, especially if their dosage is low or the administration period is short. Indeed, all patients presently under the care of a biomedical doctor should continue their treatment, even while getting treatment with Chinese medicine. When progress is made, the reduction or elimination of biomedical treatment should be done under a doctor's supervision. But not attempting to restore the body's innate ability to maintain itself is contrary to the fundamental principles behind Chinese medicine. Great importance is given to the concept behind the cliché, "Use it or lose it." The important analogy here is that the use of drugs that substitute for a function or substance will help relieve symptoms in the short term, but will lead to a weakening of function or an exhaustion of substance in the long run.

Anti-viral and neurotrophic drugs as well as analgesics are essential to the effective management of the acute attacks of herpes zoster. But biomedical techniques fail to stand up to the effectiveness of Chinese medicine when it comes to prevention and the management of post-herpetic neuralgia. Biomedical therapy alone is not enough, and is inherently incomplete.

Chinese medicine focuses on the person, who happens to be ill; rather than concentrating on the disease mechanism, which happens to be inside a person like is done in biomedicine. The methods of Chinese medicine, like other natural medical systems, are not intended to substitute for a bodily function or substance. They are intended to help the body do its job, help repair any damage, or aid in removing pathogens. When the body is healthy enough to do the job itself, treatment is no longer necessary. As an example, modern research has shown that the common herbs used for infections can not be compared to the potent antibiotics used in hospitals. Many of these herbs can only inhibit the growth of the bacteria, not destroy them. Yet experienced doctors of Chinese medicine will tell you that when properly prescribed, these herbs are effective in the management of infectious disease, and in chronic cases they are often a better choice than the standard biomedical treatment.

The underlying mechanism of the methods used is to help the body recover using natural substances and manual methods to stimulate the general functions of the body. Eventually, when the body has been "retrained" to maintain balance on its own, treatment can be reduced and then eliminated. The language it uses, qi, yin-yang, five phases, etc., is antique, but the idea it embraces is very advanced.

If you are ready to take an active role in your health and in your life, Chinese medicine is right for you.

But remember, achieving good health is not like climbing a mountain, with a visible goal, but like maintaining a garden, giving constant care and paying attention to changes in the environment. Chinese medicine has been helping transform what is sometimes seen as an arduous task into a rewarding joy for millions of people for thousands of years. If you also want your garden to thrive, come and join the community of natural medicine, learn more about Chinese medicine.

Let us start by reading about a real case before introducing the basic concepts of Chinese medicine.

Case 1

Mrs. Li, age 60, visited a Chinese doctor one day in September. She complained of painful raised red bumps on the right side of her chest and rib side that had been there for more than a week. Upon examination, the doctor found two walnut-sized skin lesions under her right rib cage, along with a large number of pea-sized bumps, all with a tight wall and red edges. Instead of taking a blood sample, her tongue and pulse were checked. She had a red tongue with a yellow coating and what the doctor described as a wiry slippery pulse. By combing all the signs and symptoms, the doctor diagnosed her as suffering from herpes zoster caused by too much heat accumulating in the muscles and skin. The doctor prescribed two herbal prescriptions, one to be taken internally, and

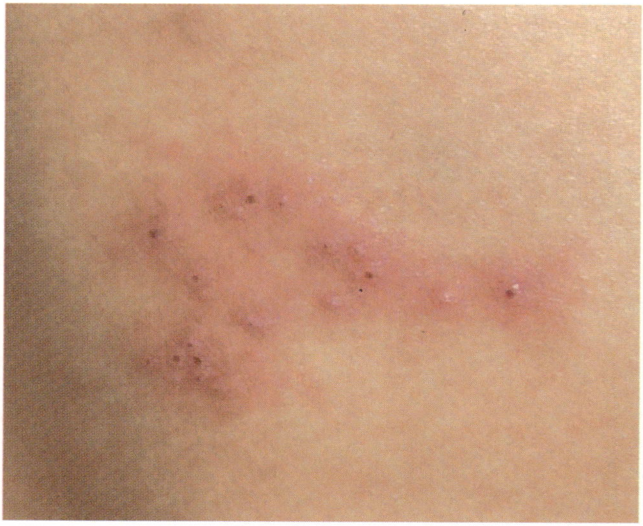

Herpes Lesions

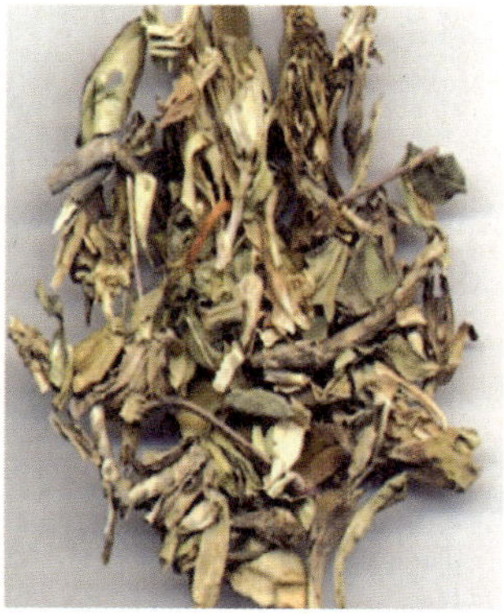

Gentian

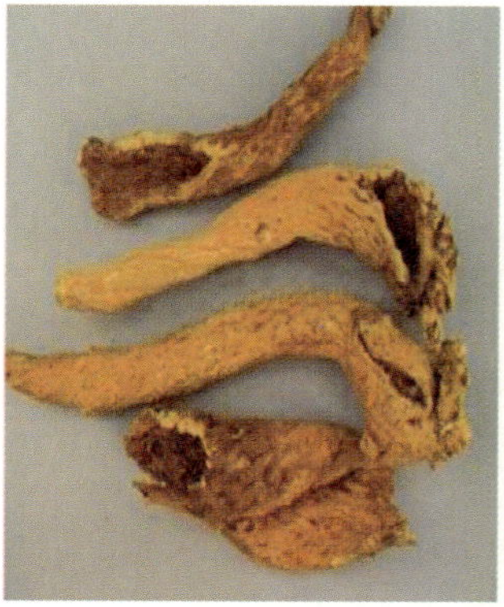

Scutellaria

another an ointment for external use. After a week's treatment, the patient happily observed that the fluid in skin lesions disappeared and began scabbing over. The pain was also significantly relieved. The patient was instructed to continue with the same prescriptions and after another week the lesions were gone and she was completely recovered[2].

Chapter 2

How Does Chinese Medicine Understand Herpes Zoster?

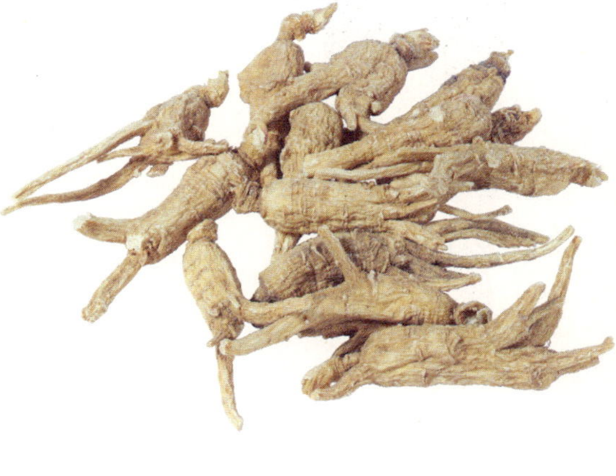

Many people in western countries are under the impression that Chinese medicine and acupuncture involve some kind of sorcery with needles or mysterious spirits. And indeed the ancient language of Chinese medicine can reinforce this view by referring to the "spirits" of the heart, lungs, liver, etc., or by insisting on the existence of the *jingluo* (channels), which is the network that runs throughout the body and is responsible for transporting qi and blood. However, to wise doctors and open-minded patients, the words used matter little, what is important is if the underlying concepts are able to be applied and beneficial results obtained.

Bronze Acupuncture Model

Introduction to Chinese Medicine

Chinese medicine enjoys a rich tradition and the longest continuous history among the world's natural medicines. Its legends suggest a history of 5,000 years, while archeological evidence dates back to 1,700 BC. The earliest existing literature dates from 200 BC and includes material from even earlier times[3]. Chinese medicine is remarkable in having not only survived, but thrived during thousands of years of political and social ups-and-downs, and in remaining relevant and continuing to grow despite the rise of biomedicine. It is presently providing safe and effective care at an increasing rate to people all over the globe.

Perhaps an illustrative example of how Chinese medicine has greatly benefited society at large will help you understand its potential value to the world. During the infamous flu epidemic of 1918 that swept over the world causing millions of deaths, the death rate in China was lower than in other countries[4]. It is estimated that over 2% of the world's population died during the flu with some countries suffering as much as a 20% loss of life[5]. The statistics for China's southern province of Guangdong, however, say only 0.1% of the population

Dao

Lao Zi

died[4]. During this time, biomedicine was largely unavailable to the vast majority of China's huge population. The people relied on the methods and theories of Chinese medicine to maintain health and treat disease. It is incredible to think that this natural system of health care was effective against one of the deadliest, most rapidly spreading diseases in the past century.

Chinese medicine is based on the traditional philosophy and culture of ancient China, the essence of which is the relationship between man, the universe, and the *dao* ("law" or "way") of nature. The *dao* of nature is a dynamic balance between yin and yang, and health is the balance between yin and yang, as well as qi and blood within the body, and between the body and the external environment. When this balance is disrupted, disease, pain, and suffering arise. The basic principle in Chinese medicine is to discover and act on the fundamental cause of the imbalance to restore harmony to yin, yang, qi and blood, i.e. the ability of the body to heal itself.

Chinese medicine is as deep as an ocean, as wide as the sky, and can seem as complex as a jungle, but it is fundamentally a natural and simple system. Everything it encompasses can be understood in terms of yin, yang, and qi. For those who approach Chinese medicine from afar, the story begins with qi.

Two Key Concepts in Chinese Medicine

1. Qi

Qi

Zhuang Zi

The concept of qi is much more than a medical term. Indeed, it is inseparable from ancient Chinese philosophy and is used by both fields to explain the forces that animate and control everything in the universe, from the cycle of seasons, to the origins and effects of emotions, to the inner workings of the human body. There is no simple literal English translation of qi. Different translators have rendered it as air, vapor, or energy and all of these are partially, but not completely, accurate.

The concept of qi is somewhat similar to pneuma in ancient Greece or prana in India, which were used to describe an underlying life force that was seen as having a strong connection to air and breath. Some of qi's important characteristics are:

- Qi is indeed a kind of life force, but it is also a tangible vital substance that makes up everything in the cosmos, including humans.
- Qi is the medium for transformation that stimulates the process of change. Everything in the universe, organic or inorganic, is made of qi and defined by qi. Mountains, rivers, animals, plants, even human emotions all have qi.
- Qi cannot be defined as simply 'energy', nor can it be labeled a mere material substance, nor is it something in between. It is what connects humankind and the natural environment.
- Qi is the media that makes the relationships and interactions between things and lives possible.

It can be difficult to understand the ancient Chinese claim that qi is both an ethereal life force as well as a material substance. To understand better, let us look at two very different categories of phenomena, human emotions and simple writing utensils, and see how qi exists in both of them.

First, take emotions. If a doctor of Chinese medicine was asked to describe the qi of the emotion of joy, he or she would probably say that its qi was light, rising, dispersing or possibly warm. On the other hand, if asked to describe the qi of fear, the words used would be more along the lines of dark, sinking, or cold. These descriptions are not based on any lab tests or scientific evidence, but are based primarily on the practitioner's own experience of the resonance between the emotional state and his or her perception.

Now let us look at the other end of the spectrum, at two examples of solid, tangible writing utensils. One a well-worn wooden pencil with teeth-marks, the kind a first grader might use to scratch out the ABC's; the other a sleek, expensive ink pen, probably black or silver that could be used to sign legal contracts. Similar to the description of joy above, the qi of the pencil could be described as light, familiar, or warm; and similar to the qi of fear above, the pen's qi would be described as dark, heavy, and cold.

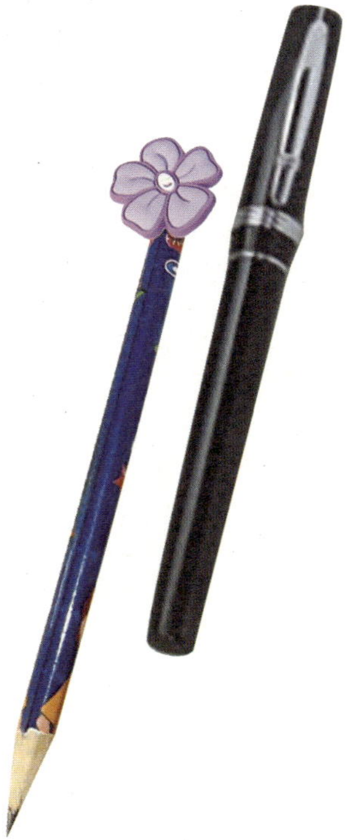

We can see that qi is not merely energy, as the physical substance of the pencils was a crucial part of describing their qi. Likewise, we saw that qi cannot be limited to physical characteristics because the emotions described above, which have their distinct qi, have no tangible substance.

Chinese medicine, over thousands of years and with the help of countless doctors, patients, and philosophers has established a system in which the different phenomena of the universe can be described by qi and likewise the relationships between these phenomena can be described. Thus a Chinese doctor, when asked to describe the qi of some thing or the other, is not merely relying on his own experience and perceptions, but is using established theories to come up with an accurate description that anyone trained in qi will be able to agree with. In fact, it does not necessarily have training to understand qi. Most people would find the metaphorical descriptions of joy, fear, the pencil, and the pen easy to relate to. All people can think and talk in terms of qi, since it is based on the common sense of the natural world. The genius of Chinese medicine lies in its clear definitions and natural categorizations.

Albert Einstein

To understand what doctors of Chinese medicine aim to do, we have to understand this well-used but rarely understood word, qi. Matter and energy are not independent of each other. As shown in Einstein's famous equation $E=mc^2$, there is an intrinsic relationship between matter and energy. Qi is a concept of both matter and energy. It is the force that animates life. It is also the matter that constitutes life. Qi is shared by everything in the universe. It is the medium by which everything interacts. To quote one of the original textbooks of Chinese medicine in English, *The Web that Has No Weaver:*

"The interaction, or resonance, is realized by qi. Health is the harmonious resonance while disease is the disharmony. Components of the universe, the qi of herbs, acupuncture points, lifestyle activities, or living environments share a resonating frequency that already exists in a person. A medicine or a conscious shift in a person's behavior can resonate with the condition within a person (e.g. a pattern of a disharmony) and induce a person toward health[6]."

In terms of the human body and its various activities, Chinese medicine describes qi as having five major functions. They are as follows:

(1) Promoting: Qi is the source of all movements.

Qi is a powerful substance that ignites and promotes all movements. Here 'movement' is in its broadest sense and includes all physiological and psychological activities: walking, dancing, breathing, the heart beating, the blood flowing, the distribution of body fluids, speaking, thinking, birth, growth, development, maturation, and aging. Qi promotes all normal functions of the human body.

(2) Warming: Qi warms the body

and is the source of the heat energy of the body.

Maintenance of normal body temperature relies on the warming function of qi. This warming function also helps to smooth the flow and distribution of blood and body fluids. This warmth is also necessary for the internal organs to maintain normal function. The warmth can be manifested as the actual body temperature, in the normal function of the organs, or as the patient's subjective feeling of hot or cold. The difference between one person's qi and another's can partly explain why some people tend to wear more clothes than others even though the temperature is the same. When qi is deficient, internal cold arises. When qi is excessive or accumulated, internal heat is generated.

(3) Defending: Qi protects the body, resisting the invasion of various external pathogens and preventing diseases.

This function is often compared to immunity in biomedicine. Harmony of qi in the body is what protects us from pathogens in our environment. A quote from the most famous text of Chinese medicine, the *The Yellow Emperor's Classic of Internal Medicine (Huáng Dì Nèi Jīng)* states, "If things from outside are able to harm the body, the qi must be weak." When qi is weak, we are vulnerable to disease. When qi is plentiful, we are less susceptible to illness. Qi can also help fight pathogens when they attack. The prognosis of disease is simply the dynamic balance sheet between the body's healthy qi and the attacking qi of the pathogenic factors.

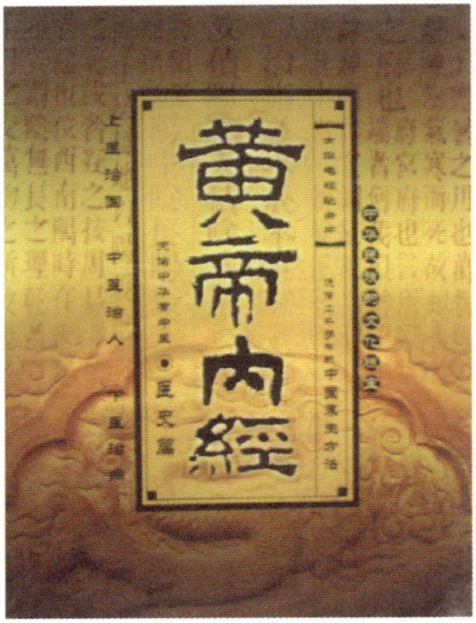

The Yellow Emperor's Classic of Internal Medicine (Huáng Dì Nèi Jīng)

(4) Securing: Qi keeps things in their proper place.

This means controlling bodily substances such as blood, urine, mucus, and saliva and preventing them from leaking out. It also describes the maintenance of the structural integrity of the body, helping to keep organs in their proper places. When this function is disrupted it will lead to problems such as bleeding or excessive secretion of body fluids, i.e. excessive sweating upon slight exertion, frequent urination, heavy bleeding during menstruation; or loss of structural integrity with proplapses of organs or body parts like is seen in uterine prolapse or various hernias.

(5) Qi-transforming: Qi is the source of transformation

Changes in the body and mind are ascribed to the transformative function of qi. This can be compared to metabolism in biomedical terminology. For example, food is digested and transformed into bodily substances. Emotional stress may influence the body and cause problems like headaches. For better or worse, these transformations are dependent on qi. Too much, too little, or improperly moving qi can cause different kinds of problems with the transformations that are managed by qi.

In summary, qi is the general force that animates the body's functions. Qi is also the material basis on which different parts of the body can interact. When our qi is healthy and plentiful, we enjoy physical and emotional well-being. This healthy qi can be easily disrupted if we don't take constant care. These disruptions can be caused by sudden weather changes, stress, unhealthy food, or lack of proper physical activity.

The qi of herpes zoster patients is often disturbed and deficient. The following graph outlines some qi disorders of herpes zoster patients:

Qi Disorders of Patients with Herpes Zoster

	Failure to promote	**Failure to warm**	**Failure to defend**	**Failure to secure**	**Failure to transform**	**Failure to nurture**
Pathological changes	Nerves impaired	Not common in herpes zoster	Decreased immunity	Leakage of fluid	Poor fluid metabolism	Undernourished skin
Symptoms and signs	Pain, Weakness, Fatigue	Not common in herpes zoster	Easy infections; Non-healing lesions	Fluid-filled lesions	Fluid-filled lesions	Coarse and itchy skin

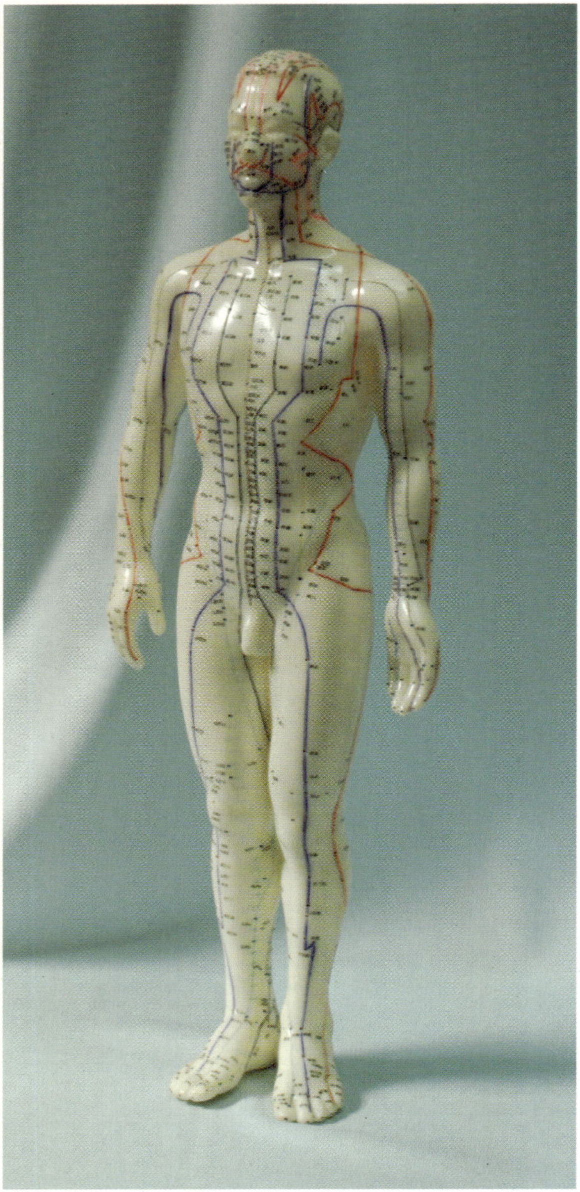

Channels on the Front

The basis of physiology, pathology, diagnosis, and treatment in Chinese medicine is the theory of essential qi. This theory's main principle is that essential qi is the basic substance that makes up the body. The physiological and pathological changes of the body are the results of normal and abnormal movements of qi respectively. Analyzing the movements of qi is an important part of diagnosis in Chinese medicine, which is called pattern differentiation. Therefore, the purpose of treatment is to adjust these abnormalities of qi.

For example, many patients with herpes zoster suffer from persistent pain which is aggravated by touch, but some experience intermittent pain that is alleviated when rubbed. Chinese medicine sees these symptoms as being caused by different qi disorders while biomedicine can't offer a satisfactory explanation. Pain, in Chinese medicine, is caused by qi blockage and stagnation.

Ginseng

In the classic *the Yellow Emperor's Classic of Internal Medicine (Huáng Dì Nèi Jīng)*, it is written, "When there is stagnation, there will be pain." Therefore, when qi accumulates in any place and doesn't move, there will be pain.

If the patient has an excess of qi, the accumulated qi can not go anywhere, it is stuck like a traffic jam and the qi is constantly stagnated and there is persistent pain. If, however, the patient does not have enough qi, the qi moves along in fits and starts, like a poorly running car, so the qi sometimes moves and sometimes is stagnated, leading to intermittent pain. But why would one patient's pain be aggravated by touch, while another's pain is relieved by rubbing? As an example, look at two gas filled balloons, one taut and full of gas and another shriveled and loose with just a little air. When you press the two balloons with the same strength you will surely feel the puffy one has a stronger reaction. Accumulated qi has a similar reaction to touch. With an excess amount of qi, the qi has no where to go when touched so touching only aggravates the

Gardenia

Rhubarb

Ginseng

stagnation. If the qi is deficient, then rubbing will quickly relieve the stagnation by pushing the qi along its proper course.

A saying in Chinese medicine also states, "Qi in excess turns to fire." Depending on the diagnosis and the nature of the pain, a practitioner might prescribe qi moving and heat clearing herbs like gardenia fruit and rhubarb root or herbs that supplement qi like ginseng and astragalus.

The meaning of qi is many faceted. Qi is what links man and nature, it is the material basis for all things. Chinese medicine has discovered that the qi of the internal organs can be reflected on the external parts of the body. The qi of heart is manifested on the tongue, the qi of the liver is manifested in the eyes, the qi of spleen (pancreas) can be seen on the mouth, while the qi of the lungs is evident on the nose, and the qi of the kidney can be observed on the ears. By observing the external manifestations, the functions of the internal organs can be inferred*. Meanwhile, stimulus received externally can be conducted into the internal organs by qi. Acupuncture, moxibustion and massage are all based on the concept that qi in the channels can act on the internal organs.

* These internal organ - sense organ correspondences may sound strange to many readers. Please remember that the Chinese understanding of organ function is different from the understanding of modern biomedicine. The organs in Chinese medicine have a variety of functions that are connected through theory and confirmed by clinical experience. Sometimes the translation of the Chinese term can cause confusion. For example, the organ which is commonly translated as "spleen" in English actually performs the functions of the pancreas and is a central organ of digestion in Chinese medicine. In fact, the original Chinese term meant neither "spleen" nor "pancreas", but defined an organ whose sphere of influence was predominant in the digestive system.

Licorice

It is the fundamental, simple concepts that are most important and often neglected in learning. The idea of qi, along with yin-yang theory, is of utmost importance to Chinese medicine. Without qi there is death; with qi there is life. Try not to form a fixed idea about qi after this short explanation. Keep an open mind and deepen your understanding of qi as we explore more about Chinese medicine.

Case 2

Mrs. Zhu, a female patient in her forties, had been suffering from herpes zoster for two months. At the beginning, she had severe stabbing pain in the left side of the lower back accompanied with dense clusters of blisters. After being treated with biomedicine, the lesions subsided, but the pain remained, and failed to respond to any drugs. Therefore, she sought help from Chinese medicine. Her most serious complaint was stabbing pain in the low back and ribcage regions. Other symptoms and signs included a loud voice, irritability, difficulty sleeping, a dry mouth with a bitter taste, dark yellow urine, constipation, a dry tongue coating, and a slightly rapid pulse. The doctor diagnosed a heat syndrome caused by an excess stagnation of qi. To deal with the pain, herbs that promote the movement of qi and clear heat were administered. After taking the herbs for only three days, her pain was significantly relieved and the other signs and symptoms were also alleviated. She continued with this therapy for another six days until the pain disappeared. She had experienced no relapses by a check-up the following year[7].

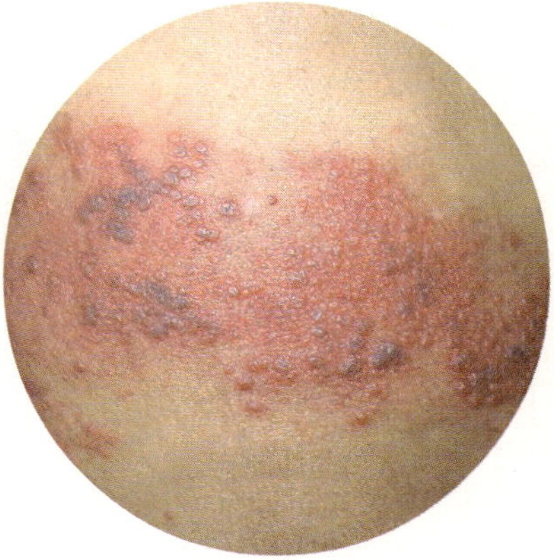

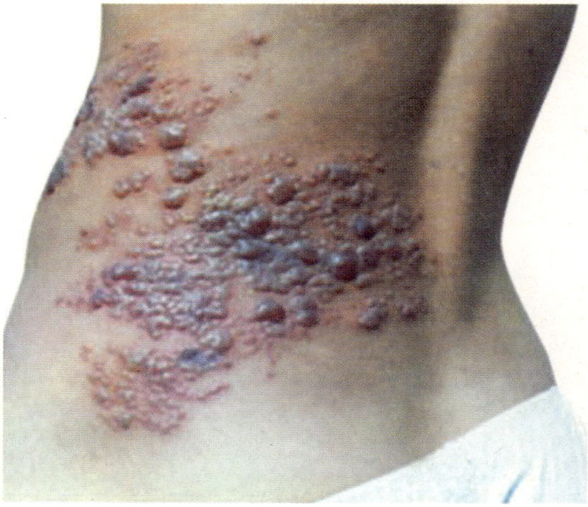

2. Yin-yang

Originally, the words yin and yang were used to describe the sides of a mountain that predominately faced away or towards the sun respectively. In other words, the side facing the sun pertains to yang while the side facing away from the sun is yin. Due to the regular rotation of the earth, each individual mountain will have one side that mostly faces the sun, which is the yang side, and one side that usually faces away from the sun, which is the yin side. Indeed because of the regular change from darkness to light due to the rotation of the earth, everything has an intrinsic yin aspect and yang aspect. The rotation of our planet has caused everything on it to evolve in such a way that it adapts to the cyclic coming of light and dark. Yin and yang are inseparable characteristics of being part of planet Earth. The concept of unified duality is a central part of ancient Chinese culture, and the Chinese understanding of every natural and social phenomenon is based on this. There are always two (with a relationship), not an isolated one. Harmony is the balance between the two.

Yin-yang of the Tai Ji

Yang is associated with such qualities as brightness and warmth while yin is associated with the opposing characteristics of darkness and cold. Some further examples are: daytime pertains to yang while night is yin; sunny weather is yang while cloudy weather is yin; spring and summer are yang and autumn and winter are yin; fire is yang while water is yin, and so on. Further expansion of this logic leads to the division of everything in the universe into yin or yang based on the quality, property, position, trend, function, or effect of the phenomena being classified.

The concept of yin-yang is the general division of any given thing (including living things, inanimate objects, feelings, actions, etc.) into two polar attributes which are related to each other. Yin and yang can also be used to subdivide already classified categories. For example, we already described summer as yang, but during summer there are days when it is extremely hot (more yang) and days when it is cloudy and cooler (more yin). The complementary and opposing nature of yin and yang can be used as labels to describe two opposing things or two opposing aspects contained within one thing. See the following table for a clearer picture of the categorization of yin and yang.

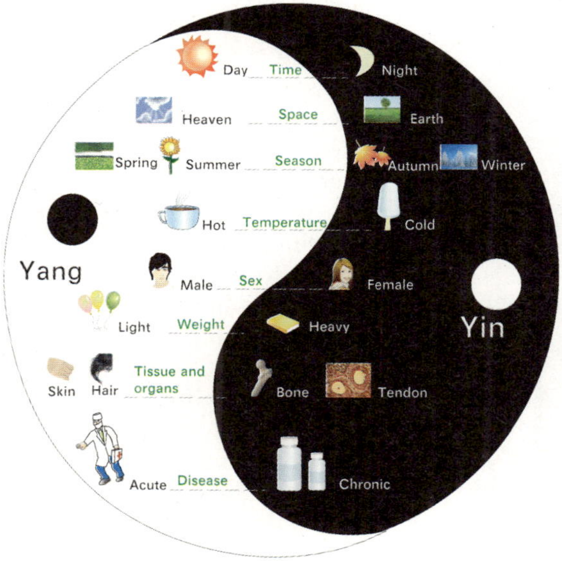

Examples of Yin-yang Categorization

In Chinese medicine the fundamental definition of health is when there is a good balance of yin and yang in the body. Diagnosis of disease and its management are all aimed at restoring this equilibrium. This may sound simplistic, but when you consider the fact that all organs, functions, emotions, fluids, and structures each have yin and yang aspects that must be balanced, you can see how the doctor's job of detecting every imbalance with using no more than the five senses is a very difficult task!

Yin and yang are inter-dependent. This means that the condition of one will affect the other. If there is too little yin, then yang will appear to be in excess; and if there is too much yin, there will appear to be too little yang. The reverse is of course true for when there is too little or too much yang. A simple example can be seen when the body's temperature rises or falls too much. With fever there is a relative abundance of yang heat. This means the cool yin aspect of the body is not sufficient to counteract the heat. Therefore the practitioner must restore the balance of yin and yang by making the cool yin aspect of the body equal to the hot yang aspect. Likewise, if a patient has hypothermia and has dangerously low body temperature there is a relative abundance of yin cold in relation to yang heat.

However, it is not enough to know merely which is the stronger of yin or yang and which is the weaker. If there is more yang than yin, for example, this could be due to either too much yang and thus yin is relatively weak, or it could be because there is not enough yin and therefore yang only appears to be in excess.

This is a difficult concept for all beginning students of Chinese medicine so let us look at an example. A forest that has not had any rain for many months will be dry and probably hot. Dryness and heat are yang qualities as opposed to yin moisture and cold. A forest that is on fire is also in a condition of yang heat. In each case, the yang aspect is greater than the yin aspect. But to restore the yin-yang balance of both situations, one must choose different strategies. To restore the forest in drought it is necessary to add yin, meaning water. On the other hand, to balance a blazing fire, one has no other option but to remove the excess yang fire. In Chinese medicine, the dry forest would be said to be in a state of yin deficiency, where the heat is due to a relative abundance of yang. The forest fire is a state of yang excess, where yin may very well be normal. The other states are yang deficiency and yin excess. Please see the diagrams to better understand the four different types of yin-yang imbalances.

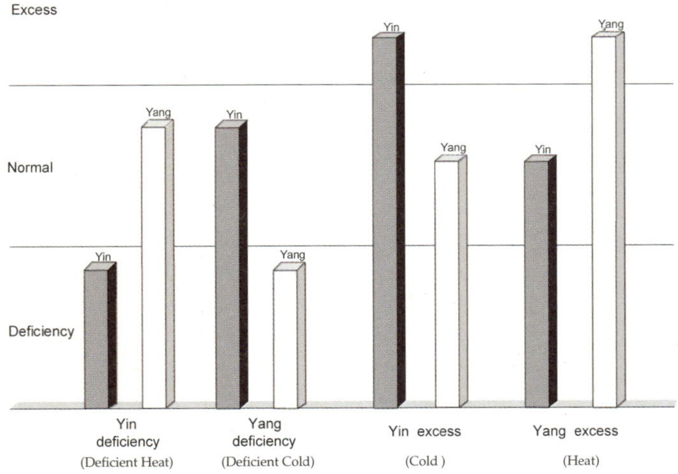

Ying-yang Disorders

*This is only a simplied model to help you understand. Remember, Yin and yang are always a pair.

The Four Different Types of Yin-yang Imbalances

	Typical manifestations
Yang excess	Fever, aversion to heat, thirst, desire for cold drinks, reddish complexion, restlessnes, yellowish-colored mucus, dark-colored urination, constipation, red tongue, yellowish tongue coating, rapid pulse
Yin excess	Aversion to cold, no thirst, desire for warm drinks, thin and watery mucus, loose stool, pale complexion, light-colored tongue, whitish tongue coating, slow or tense pulse
Yang deficiency	Preference for warmth, cold limbs, pale complexion, spontaneous sweating, fatigue, shortness of breath, loose stool, enlarged and light-colored tongue, whitish tongue coating, deep, slow and weak pulse
Yin deficiency	Thirst, dry mouth and throat, hot feeling in the soles and palms, afternoon fever, night sweating, red tongue with little coating, rapid and fine pulse

Diagnosis in Chinese medicine is much more dynamic than in biomedicine. Conditions may change daily, though with chronic disease it is usually safe to reevaluate once a week or so.

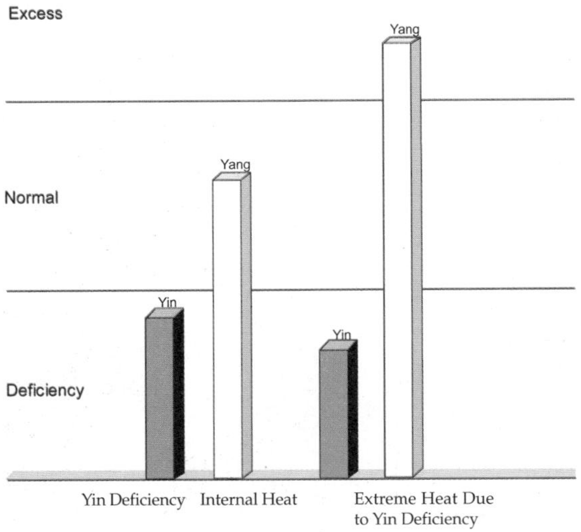

Deficient Heat

For patients with herpes zoster, the typical pathogenesis in Chinese medicine is heat in the liver and gallbladder channels (the channel system is an important part of Chinese medicine and will be illustrated later). However, the heat in some patients is caused by a yang excess, while in others it is caused by deficient yin leading to heat from a relative excess of yang. The type of heat that appears is mostly due to the underlying constitution of a person. In general, a person with a strong constitution will have heat of an excess type when ill; a person with a weaker constitution will suffer from heat of a deficient type.

In either case the heat is due to the body's yang going to the body's exterior to fight the invading virus. This battle will gradually consume the body's resources just like a battle will consume resources and human lives. The ferocity of the battle will depend on both the strength of the body's defense and of the attacking pathogen.

A person may be born with a tendency to yin deficiency or it might be acquired through life habits. Improper diet and disturbed emotions will disrupt qi flow. This stagnation will cause internal fire. To understand how stagnant qi produces fire, think of a traffic jam in a narrow tunnel. All those engines (qi) will start to heat the place up if they don't move. Fire will then consume qi (as a flame exhausts oxygen) as well as yin. So both qi and yin have been damaged.

In clinic every patient may present with a different syndrome, or usually a combination of syndromes, because every patient is different. Even for one patient, depending on the development of the disease, life-style modifications adopted, or environmental changes, the diagnosis will also have to be modified and refined at each specific stage.

The diagnosis of yin or yang is based on an integrative and insightful analysis of all the symptoms and signs of each individual patient.

After all of the information about a patient is collected, the data will be vigorously analyzed and categorized by an experienced practitioner into different patterns of disharmony. The patterns can be numerous, and will vary with the individual, time, location, climate and other factors involved. Corresponding protocols will be decided on the specific patterns identified. Chinese medicine gives highly individualized treatment, the goal of all types of medicine. Chinese medicine's goal is the recovery of the innate function of the body, a true medicine.

Note: Five phase theory is also an important fundamental element of Chinese medicine. For herpes zoster we have chosen to focus on qi and yin-yang. Please refer to other books in this series or to the suggested reading list for more information on this aspect of Chinese medicine.

Mint

Case 3

A female patient, 77 years of age, came to visit a practitioner of Chinese medicine. She complained of distention and pain in the left chest and back, and had developed herpes lesions with red blisters six days before. Her other symptoms were fatigue, difficulty sleeping, irritability, a bitter taste in mouth, poor appetite, and dark yellow urine. Upon examination the herpes lesions were pink around the base of the blisters and she also had a red tongue with scanty coating, and a slippery thin pulse.

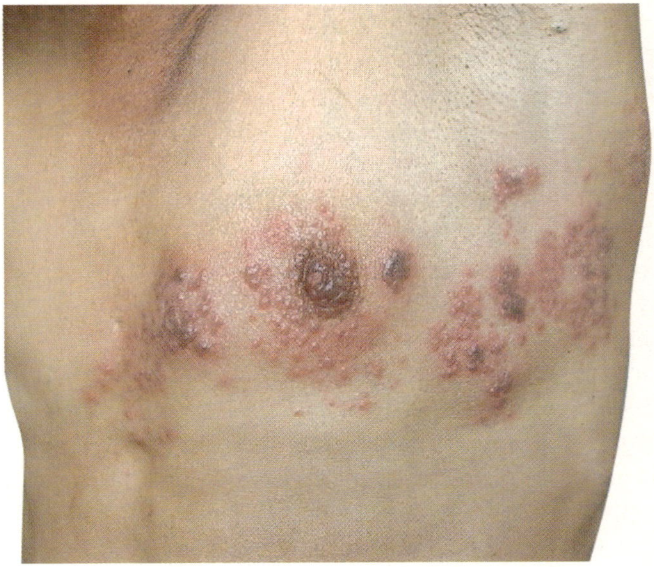

The Chinese medical pattern diagnosis was yin deficiency with stagnated heat. As people grow old, the organs and bodily functions decline. This means that qi and yin are both used up according to the theory of Chinese medicine. In this case, the elderly patient suffered from fatigue, difficulty in sleeping, and poor appetite, which are all due to qi and yin deficiency. Because yin is deficient, the yang will be relatively predominant and heat signs will appear. Heat of a yin deficient type is like a smoldering straw pile, though there is no obvious fire, it still gives out heat. It is not as intense as a raging fire, but it may last for a long time. Manifestations such as irritability, a bitter taste in mouth, dark yellow urine, and a red tongue are all indications of the presence of heat. In addition, pink color around the base of the herpes lesions indicates the heat is not too intense (deep red lesions indicate more intense heat).

According to the diagnosis, yin nourishing and heat clearing herbs were administered. After taking two packages of the herbs the patient felt relief from the pain and the skin lesions receded. She continued for another three packages of herbs after which she had recovered completely[7].

Herpes Zoster in Chinese Medicine

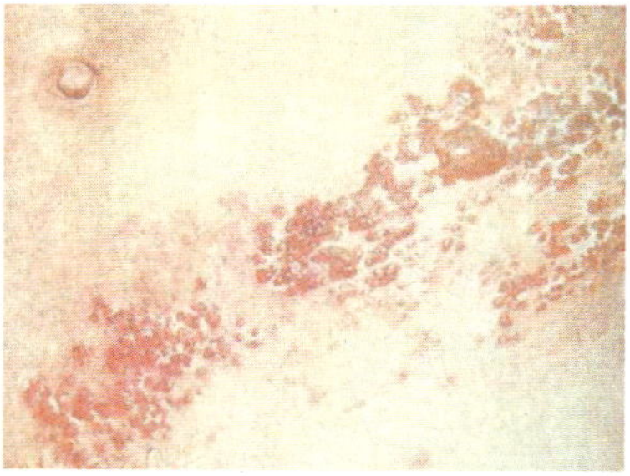

In biomedicine, herpes zoster, commonly known as shingles, is the reactivation of the varicella zoster virus (the virus that causes chickenpox) leading to an eruption of painful blisters over the dermatome of the nerve affected (the dormant virus resides in a segment of the spinal cord). Most cases involve elderly or middle aged people. It usually strikes during the spring or autumn and after a short disease course, people generally have no reoccurrence after recovery. Because herpes zoster mostly occurs in the lumbar region and back with a belt-like distribution, traditional names for the disease include *shé chuàn chuāng* (snake crawling blisters), *chán yāo lóng* (twisted dragon's waist) or *zhī zhū chuāng* (spider blisters).

The earliest record of herpes zoster in ancient Chinese medical literature was in the *Discussion of the Origins of the Symptoms of Disease (Zhū Bìng Yuán Hóu Lùn)*, written in the Sui dynasty (581-618 A.D.), and states, "There are patients with belt-like blisters twisting around the waist. Its name comes from its belt-like shape." Another classic text, the *Standards of External Medicine (Yáng Yī Zhǔn Shén)* asks, "What is the blister that looks like string of pearls surrounding the waist? It is *huǒ dài chuāng* (flaming-belt blisters), or *chán yāo huǒ dān* (flaming pellets entwining the waist)." Finally, the *Complete Collection of External Medicine (Wài Kē Dà Chéng)* recorded, "*Shé chuàn chuāng* (snake crawling blisters), which is the popular name, initially occurs in the lumbar region looking like a purplish red rope. It may turn into water blisters with severe burning pain." As can be seen, herpes zoster is very familiar to Chinese medicine[8].

Chinese medical theory sees herpes zoster as an invasion of external pathogens, namely damp and heat. In general, Chinese medicine recognizes six climatic phenomena that when excessive can cause disease: wind, cold, fire or heat, dampness, dryness, and summer-heat. When the body is weak or yin and yang are imbalanced, one or more of these six phenom of these can invade the body and cause disease. Usually, disease caused by an invasion of an external pathogen comes on suddenly, with no warning.

Both environmental and emotional factors play an important part in health and illness. The emotions are generally categorized into seven groups: joy, anger, anxiety, sorrow, thought, fear, and fright. Of course, emotions are not in themselves pathological, and all of them appear naturally in healthy individuals. It is only when an emotion is either excessive or insufficient over a long period of time, or when it arises very suddenly with great force, that it can generate imbalance and illness. The reverse is also true, physical illness can generate unbalanced emotional states.

When the human body is attacked by pathogenic dampness, heat, wind and fire, and they accumulate in the body, blocking channels and collaterals, the result will be a stagnation of qi and blood. Alternately, there may be an imbalance of the emotions leading to stagnant qi in the channels. This stagnation will eventually transform into heat.

The disease may be generated externally or internally, but often people that already have heat and stagnation internally are predisposed to easy invasion from pathogenic heat and wind. In any case, heat and fire flow to the body surface and wander through channels and collaterals. The combination of heat, wind, and dampness along with stagnated qi and blood manifest as redness, sores, blisters, itching and pain. The exact mechanism of each disease is slightly different, depending on the strength of the patient's internal condition and the power of the invading pathogens[9].

Chinese medicine gives priority to pattern differentiation. This is the way that Chinese medicine categorizes, understands, and manages all types of illnesses. It is a highly individualized principle and is always integrated with the disease diagnosis.

Peucedanum

So what is a pattern?

A pattern, similar to the concept of syndrome, is a group of interrelated signs and symptoms that together reveal the fundamental characteristics of a patient's condition. Chinese medicine believes that manifestations (symptoms and signs) mirror the performance of internal organs. So a pattern is the reflection of an underlying pathomechanism, often called the root of the disease in Chinese medicine. Over thousands of years, Chinese medicine has accumulated a large amount of experience in summarizing and categorizing these patterns in the most innovative ways. It now uses them as guidelines in prescribing treatment. Disease diagnosis and pattern diagnosis go together and guide the practitioner to the proper strategy. There is a saying in Chinese medicine, "Different diseases, same treatment; same disease, different treatment." This saying underscores the importance to individualized pattern diagnosis in Chinese medicine.

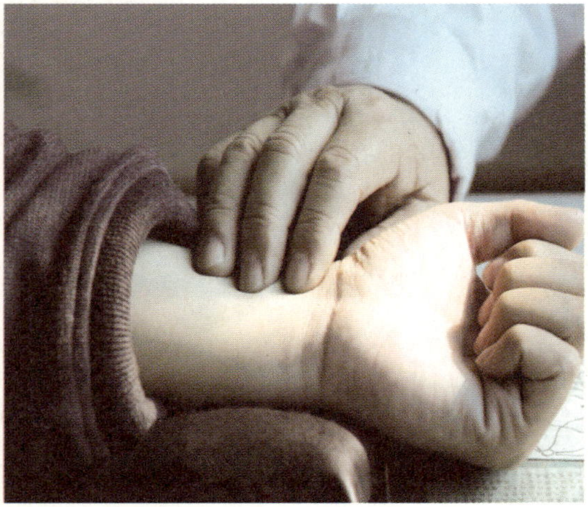

The three most common patterns that appear in herpes zoster are as follows:

Excess fire in the liver and gallbladder channels

Excess fire refers to an abundance of yang without a deficiency of yin. The connection to the liver and gallbladder does not just relate to the internal organs, but also their functions and their channels. The channels both traverse the waist and rib side areas. Also, since the liver is responsible for the smooth flow of qi in the body, there is a strong connection between the emotions and this organ, especially emotions like anger and irritability.

The heat and stagnation along the liver and gallbladder channels often manifest as marked deep red skin lesions, blisters with tense walls, and are distributed around the waist and rib side. These signs are usually accompanied by burning and stabbing pain, a bitter taste in mouth, dry throat, fidgeting and irritability, constipation with dry stool, scanty and dark yellow urine, a red tongue with yellow tongue coating, and a slippery or wiry rapid pulse. This pattern is especially noted for the intense, burning pain.

Dampness and heat in the spleen and stomach

This pattern is commonly seen among people with weak constitutions and in children. The spleen and stomach are in charge of digestion and are central to the healthy qi of the body. If the spleen and stomach are weakened by poor eating habits then they will fail to digest food properly and dampness will accumulate internally. The weakened condition combined with internal dampness makes patients especially susceptible to invasion from external damp and heat. Cases of herpes zoster mainly caused by dampness tend to be less severe, but may last longer and be more difficult to eliminate completely.

In this pattern the chief manifestations are pale red skin lesions with loose blister walls that are easily broken and often pus filled. They are mostly distributed in the abdomen and on the lower limbs, accompanied by numb and burning pain that is not as severe as the pain in cases of excess fire of the liver and gallbladder channels. Other common signs and symptoms include a greasy feeling in mouth, thirst without a strong desire to drink, poor appetite, bloating after meals, soft stool or unsmooth bowel movements, a sticky and thick tongue coating, and a slippery rapid pulse. Strengthening the digestive system is very important with this pattern.

Qi stagnation and blood stasis

Qi stagnation simply means the blockage or disruption of the normal movement of qi. Stagnation can have many causes and this pattern is present

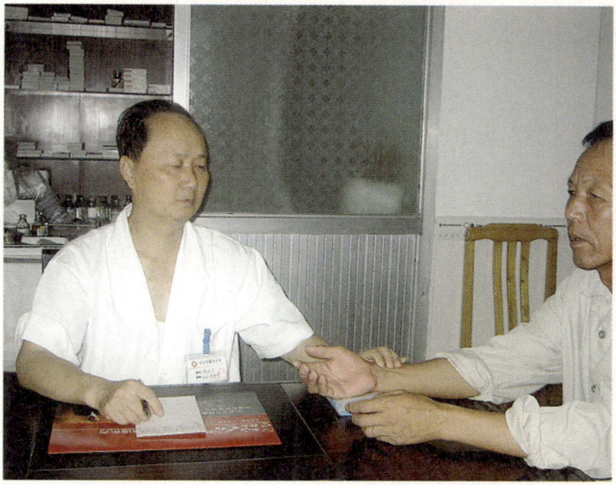

in most herpes zoster patients in at least some form. Qi and blood have a close relationship and stagnation of one can lead to stagnation of the other. In addition, external pathogens, poor diet, lack of physical activity, and emotional imbalances can contribute to the stagnation of qi and blood.

In this pattern, the chief manifestations are herpes lesions that are dark purple or reddish purple at the base, blood-filled vesicles, or vesicles that have left scabs or scars. This is often accompanied by pain in the skin, listlessness, difficulty sleeping, fidgeting, a dark purplish tongue, and a wiry pulse. This pattern is especially prominent among cases of postherpetic neuralgia.

In clinic, patients will often present with other patterns or a combination of the above patterns. The point of this division is to highlight the major symptoms and the reason for them. Treatment will be different for each pattern and each patient. Practitioners will decide how to vary treatment according to the diversity and severity of the symptoms.

Chapter 3

How Can Herpes Zoster Be Prevented?

How can the balance of yin and yang be maintained in daily life?

As explained, all natural phenomena have yin and yang aspects, and there is a constant interaction between the human body and the natural environment. The balance is easily affected by the food you eat, your lifestyle choices, the amount of exercise and rest you get, and how you manage your emotions. Your genetic predisposition also plays a role. It is important to understand your constitution and how to protect and nourish your individual condition.

The maintenance of psychological health is important but beyond the scope of this book. Chinese medicine stresses the importance of a peaceful mind for the prevention of disease. Emotional extremes most often lead to the formation of heat or fire which will eventually damage yin and exhaust qi. Maintaining a balanced diet and getting regular exercise will go a long way to maintaining a calm mind.

Diet

> Let food be your medicine and medicine be your food.
> -Hippocrates

Dietary therapy is essential to patients with herpes zoster according to both biomedicine and Chinese medicine. Without proper management of your diet, most treatment will be less effective. A classic Chinese medical text, *Basic Questions (Sù Wèn)* stated, "While herbs are used for removing pathogenic factors, grains are for nourishment, fruits for assistance, animal products for benefiting, and vegetables to supplement, all of which together reinforce the essential qi." This means that recovery from a disease requires proper diet. In general, patients with herpes zoster should eat simple and bland food that is easy to digest, enjoy fresh fruits and vegetables to gain a diversity of nutrition, especially those are rich in Vitamin B and C, and drink plenty of water. On the other hand, it is recommended to avoid spicy, greasy, fried, cold, and most sea foods, as these tend to increase damp and heat in the body. Since every individual is different, Chinese dietary therapy, which is modified according to different circumstances, offers many choices.

1. Essentials of Chinese Dietary Theory

Chinese medicine holds that food is the best medicine. The things we eat are natural substances that have their own unique qi (properties) just like Chinese medicinals. The properties of Chinese medicinals are used to correct any imbalance of qi, blood, yin, or yang. The properties of food can be used in a similar way. As much as possible, it is better to use food as medicine rather than taking any kind of medication, be it Chinese medicinals or pharmaceuticals. Eating is the most convenient, economic, and delicious prescription a doctor can administer!

Chinese dietary theory is based on the same principles of herbal medicine. Each food has its own property and is selected based on the patient's pattern to treat disease or preserve health. Western nutritional therapy, a relatively young science, separates food by content: carbohydrates, protein, fat, vitamins, etc. Chinese medicine concentrates on the qualities of each food item, dividing foods into the categories of taste and temperature. As an example, biomedicine would put most grains in the same category due to their high carbohydrate content. Chinese medicine, while also recognizing familiar food categories like grains, meat, vegetables, etc., divides grains into different categories based on their temperature and taste. Looking at food from the Chinese perspective, beef, onions, and walnuts are all considered warm. Biomedicine on the other hand, would find little in common with these three foods.

According to Chinese medical theory, every food can be categorized as having one of the four qi (hot, warm, cool, and cold) and one or more of the five flavors (sour, bitter, sweet, spicy, and salty). This classification of foods follows the same criteria used for medicinals and the application of foods follows the same diagnostic principles and procedures as well. Foods act on the internal organs and influence the qi of the body, which can be used to preserve health and manage disease. The main difference between food and medicinal substances is that food is generally milder when compared with Chinese medicinals. That's why food is taken daily and medicinals only when necessary.

To eat a balanced diet, in terms of Chinese medicine, is to balance the qi of the food. A diet too lopsided in one direction or the other for too long will eventually cause an imbalance of qi, blood, yin and/or yang. For those already suffering from disease, special foods are chosen based on the patient's individual condition. Dietary prescriptions in Chinese medicine are made according to pattern identification. Biomedicine calculates the calories, vitamins, fat content, etc. precisely. When combined with Chinese dietary theory, people can have a very well-designed dietary regimen.

Since herpes zoster in Chinese medicine often involves an accumulation of heat and dampness, patients should try their best to avoid any food with the above properties, such as most spices and seasonings, red meat, fried foods, and fish. In order to dissipate the accumulation of dampness and heat, it is recommended to eat mainly neutral or cool natured food that is light and easy to digest. Most green vegetables are very suitable for herpes zoster patients and most fruit is cool or neutral. While fruit is ok to be eaten raw, vegetables should be cooked as it is easier on the digestive system. Wheat products in small amounts are ok, but the typical modern diet has far too many calories coming from wheat products. Rice or rice porridge is mild and bland and can strengthen the spleen and stomach to dispel dampness.

Properly chosen, food can be used as medicine. Some Chinese medicinals can be used as food and added into your diet. Indeed, many common spices (cinnamon, cardamom, ginger, garlic) are commonly used in herbal medicine. In Chinese medicine, the line between food and medicine is a blurry one. Hot foods like peppers and chilies have a warming effect on the body, while cold foods like tomatoes and bananas can cool the body. Neutral foods don't have much influence on the body, and are an important part of maintaining a healthy balance. For example, rice is neutral and thus can be consumed daily, providing nourishment while not having a drastic effect on the body's function.

The following table is an example of some common foods and their properties. A complete list of the properties of foods is beyond the scope of this book. We hope that the list will

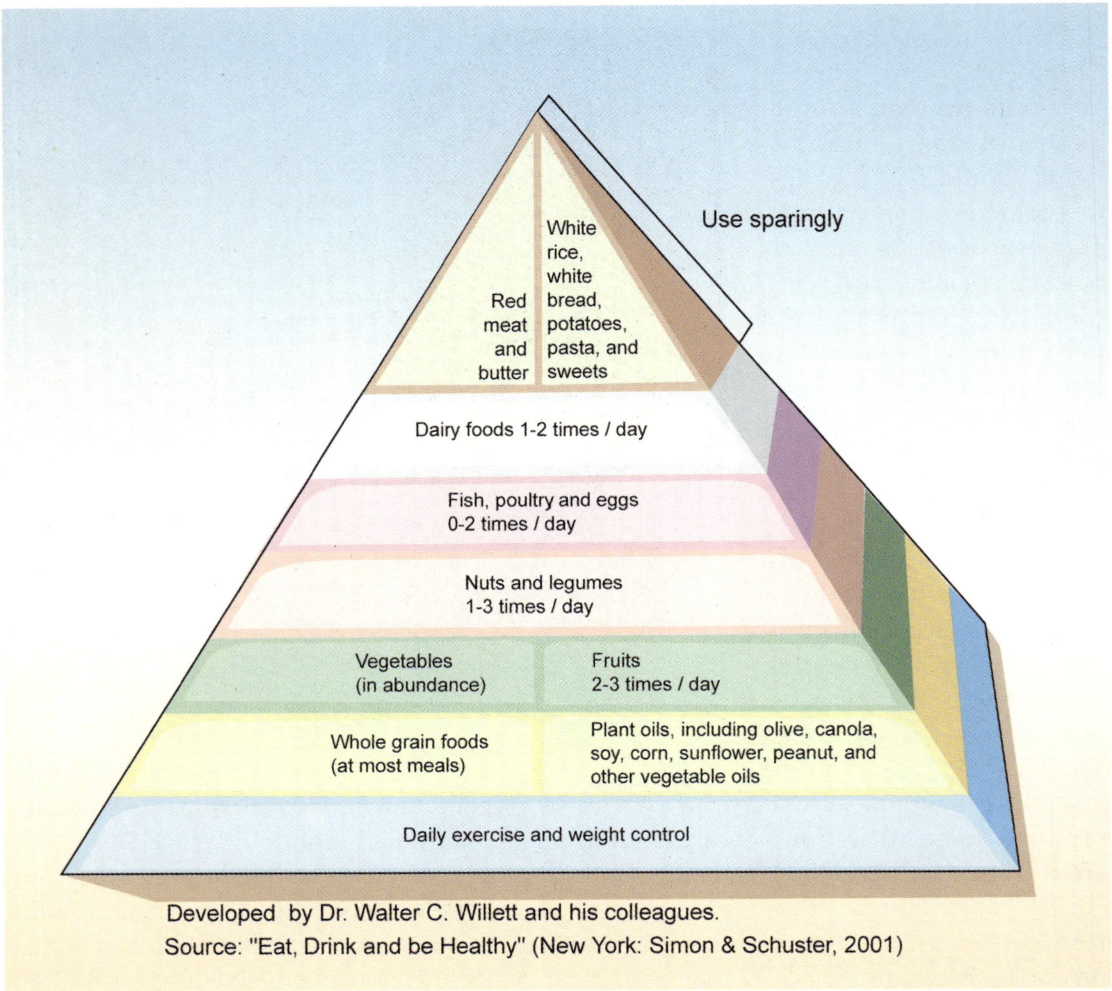

Alternative Food Pyramid

provide a good general outline, and help you make educated guesses about unlisted foods by comparing them to related items on the list. For instance, a grain that is not listed on the table could be assumed to be somewhere between neutral and cool due to the natures of the grains listed.

Common Foods and Their Properties

Category	Hot	Warm	Neutral	Cold	Cool
Function	Increase yang, speed up qi, warm up the body. These items tend to increase heat and injure yin fluid.	Strengthen yang, warm the qi and organs.	Build up qi and body fluids. Stabilize and harmonize the body.	Cool internal heat. Calm down the spirit.	Slow down qi, clear heat, and supplement body fluids.
Beverages	Alcohol	Cocoa coffee, wine			Black tea, fruit juice, pepper-mint tea
Condiments			Honey	Salt, soy source	
Dairy		Butter, goat cheese	Cheese	Cow's milk	Yogurt
Animal Products	Lamb	Beef, chicken eel, salmon	Carp, duck, egg, pork, goose	Shrimp, crayfish	Rabbit
Fruit and vegetables		Cherry, fennel, leek, peach, onion	Carrot, cauliflower, grape, fig, plum, potato	Asparagus, banana, orange, rhubarb, seaweed, tomato, watermelon	Celery, cucumber, soy bean, sprouts, spinach, zucchini
Grains and legumes			Corn, lentil, millet, peas, rice, spelt		Barley, tofu, wheat
Herbs and spices	Cinnamon, chili, curry, garlic, ginger, paprika, pepper				

(The table is adapted from I-23, Joweh Kastner. Chinese Nutrition Therapy. Theme Stuttgart, New York, 2004)

The flavors of foods are associated with the internal organs, and influence them just like medicinals do. The essence of Chinese dietary therapy is to make proper food choices and add medicinals into the diet that will help to restore your body's harmony.

2. Specifics and Recipes for Herpes Zoster

Everyday eating

In everyday life it is important to eat food that is good for the digestive system and avoid food that can generate dampness. This is especially true for anyone who has a disease that is associated with weak digestion or dampness. To avoid dampness it is better to eat only small amounts of the following: fish, shrimp, crab, egg, milk, shallot, pepper, leek, and mustard. Ingredients that help the spleen and stomach and remove dampness can be eaten heartily: gourds and pumpkins, bean sprout, yam, lily, wild rice, tofu, and pork. Suitable cooking methods include: light frying, stewing, and steaming, but never with too heavy a flavor. Other acceptable foods are many types of bean, corn or barley, watermelon, pear, star fruit, cherry, strawberry, and oranges. If a patient suffers from yin deficiency or fluid dryness they should choose yin nourishing products: spinach, cabbage, mushrooms, yam, pork, and duck. It is also good to eat a lot of

fresh fruits like coconut, peach, plum, lychee, pineapple, and strawberry.

For patients with excessive heat, the patient should not eat much spicy or heavily flavored food. This includes coffee, strong tea, wine, milk, eggs, shrimp, eel, onion, hot peppers, pepper, leeks and garlic. It is better to select mild fruits and vegetables like squash, cabbage, sprouts, pear, cucumber, lettuce, lotus root, and beans. Suitable cooking methods include stewing and steaming, but not frying in oil, stir frying and baking. In addition, most spices like onions, hot peppers, pepper, garlic, dried ginger, cinnamon and cooking wine are hot and may boost internal heat. These thus should be avoided or used infrequently. Eat freely of fresh fruits like watermelon, pears, oranges, and grapefruit[10].

Special items for herpes zoster

The following items are specially recommended for patients with herpes zoster. Many of these items are not common to the western diet, but because they are so helpful in the management of disease, patients are strongly advised to find these wonderful foods and integrate them into their diets. Many of them can be found in Asian supermarkets or natural food stores. Some of them are available in concentrated form as pills or powders. In order to help you find them, we have tried to include various common names, as well as the Chinese characters.

Purslane (马齿苋)

Cold in nature and sour in taste, purslane is common at dinner tables throughout Asia. Indeed it was said to be Ghandi's favorite food. It is commonly seen as a weed and can be collected in the summer and autumn when the stem and leaves are tender and succulent. Purslane is easily prepared in salads, sautéed lightly, or in soups. Chopped fresh purslane can be applied directly on painful skin lesions to soothe inflammation. Besides being able to clear heat and remove toxins, purslane is high in essential Omega-3 fatty acids. Many people grow their own purslane, though it can be found in supermarkets.

Propolis (蜂胶)

A resinous substance used by bees in their hives, the name derives from the Greek, and means "protection of the city" implying it can strengthen body resistance and fight invaders. It is well known throughout Europe, where it has been used for many years. Many studies have shown that propolis extracts are able to kill the herpes zoster virus as well as diminish inflammation and relieve pain. It can be taken internally or applied externally. It can be very beneficial over only a short period of time. Propolis can usually be found in the vitamin and supplement section of natural food stores.

Jasmine (茉莉花)

Famous for its fragrance, jasmine is widely known and grown all over the world. It favors warm and moist areas, and grows best in shady, airy places. It can be taken as a tea or cooked with other ingredients. Jasmine can resolve stagnant qi and blood and help relieve pain.

Dandelion (蒲公英)

This everyday weed that "parachutes" over fields and yards in the summer is mild in nature and slightly bitter in taste. It can be steeped and taken as tea daily, or taken in capsule form. Dandelion can reduce inflammation, clear heat and remove toxins. Most health food stores will sell extracts of dandelion.

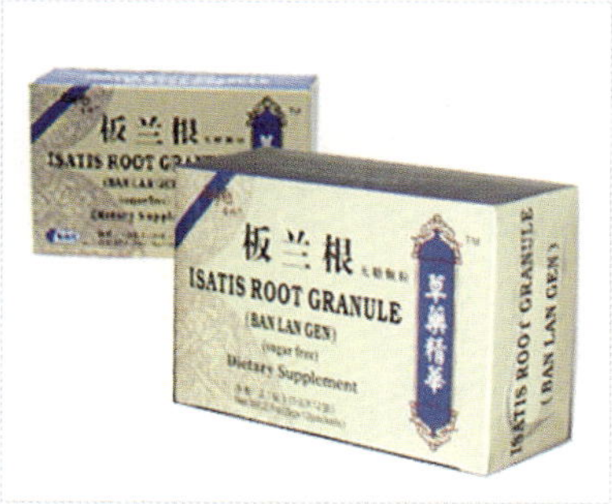

Isatis Root (板蓝根)

Cold in nature and bitter in taste, it is effective in clearing heat, removing toxins, and cooling blood. The raw form can be boiled and drunk as a tea, but it is commonly found in health food stores in pill or extract form. This herb has marked anti-viral properties and is a common ingredient in cold and flu remedies in China.

Recipes for different patterns

Below are some suggestions on medicinal ingredients that can be used in simple recipes plus common foods that are good for herpes zoster. Most of the medicinals cited are sweet flavored or fairly bland so they won't impart a very strong taste to the dishes. Most of them are best used in soups and stews, though more specific cooking information is listed in the recipes. The patterns listed below are simple ones and a patient may have two or more of the patterns mentioned below. If that is the case, please choose freely from any recipe that pertains to your pattern. We hope that with the advice of your practitioner, you can learn which recipes and ingredients are right for you and incorporate them into your daily routine. Since many of the medicinals listed will only be available from an herbalist, please see the list below for the names of the ingredients in Chinese.

The measurements in these recipes are listed in grams, 30 grams is roughly equivalent to one ounce.

1) Lycium fruit porridge

Cook 30g lycium fruit with 50g rice into porridge. Eat a bowl of the porridge every morning and evening.

This recipe can clear heat and purge liver fire. It is suitable for cases of herpes zoster with excessive fire in the liver and gallbladder.

2) Coix seed porridge

Cook 30-60g of coix seed with some rice into a soft porridge. Season with sea salt or brown sugar, depending on your preference.

This recipe is suitable for all types of herpes zoster, especially for those with dampness and heat in the spleen and stomach.

3) Coix seed and lablab bean porridge

Cook 30g coix seed and 30g lablab bean into a soft porridge. Eat a bowl once a day for at least a week.

This recipe can strengthen the spleen and remove dampness. It is suitable for herpes zoster patients with dampness and heat in the spleen and stomach.

4) Purslane porridge

Cook 100-200g cleaned and sliced purslane with a proper amount of rice into a loose porridge. A small amount of sea salt can be added for flavoring.

This recipe is suitable for two types of herpes zoster: excessive heat in the liver and gallbladder channels, and dampness and heat in the spleen and stomach.

5). Isatis leaf and Bupleurum root porridge

The ingredients are 15g isatis leaf, 15g bupleurum root, 30g rice, and a proper amount of sugar. Boil the isatis leaf and buplenrum root in 3 cups of water until 2 cups remain. Remove the dregs and then cook the liquid, rice and sugar together into a loose porridge. Eat a bowl a day for 5 or 6 days.

This recipe can help move stagnant qi and clear heat. It is suitable for herpes zoster due to excess heat in the liver and gallbladder[11].

6). Codonopsis root, Chinese angelica and pork chop soup

The ingredients are 30g codonopsis root, 30g Chinese angelica and 500g pork chops. Wrap the codonopsis root and Chinese angelica in cheese cloth, and stew it with the pork chop and some water until the chop is extremely soft and season according to taste. Eat a bowl of the soup and meat once a day for 3 to 5 days.

This recipe can strengthen qi and nourish blood. It is suitable for cases of herpes zoster that are slow to recover and patients with deficient qi and blood.

7) Chinese angelica and Buddha's hand fruit tea

The ingredients are 6g Chinese angelica, 30g Buddha's hand fruit, and 30ml rice wine. Boil the ingredients in two cups of water for about 30 minutes. Drink the remaining liquid once a day for 3-5 days.

This recipe can soothe qi flow, nourish blood and invigorate blood circulation. It is suitable for herpes zoster with qi stagnation and blood stasis.

8) Notoginseng and Chaenomeles fruit wine

The ingredients are 15g notoginseng, 35g chaenomeles fruit, and 500ml liquor (rice wine). Put the notoginseng and chaenomeles fruit in to the liquor, seal, and store in a cool dark place for 15 days. Take a small glass every day.

This beverage is suitable for post-herpetic neuralgia due to qi and blood stagnation[12].

The following table gives you the common, Chinese, and Latin names of the ingredients mentioned above.

Ingredient Names

Common Name	Latin Name	Pinyin	Chinese
Coix seed	Semen Coicis	*yì yǐ rén*	薏苡仁
Lablab bean	Semen Lablab Album	*bái biǎn dòu*	白扁豆
Purslane	Herba Portulacae	*mǎ chǐ xiàn*	马齿苋
Isatis leaf	Folium Isatidis	*dà qīng yè*	大青叶
Bupleurum root	Radix Bupleuri	*chái hú*	柴胡
Codonopsis root	Radix Codonopsis	*dǎng shēn*	党参
Chinese angelica	Radix Angelicae Sinensis	*dāng guī*	当归
Notoginseng	Radix et Rhizoma Notoginseng	*sān qī*	三七
Chaenomeles fruit	Fructus Chaenomelis	*mù guā*	木瓜
Buddha's hand fruit	Fructus Sacrodactylis	*fó shǒu gān*	佛手柑
Lycium fruit	Fructus Lycii	*gǒu qǐ*	枸杞

Daily Habits

Besides an appropriate diet, there are other aspects of daily life that demand special attention as well. These suggestions will be very helpful in preventing or dealing with an attack of herpes zoster.

- Pay attention to climate changes and always wear proper clothing according to the weather. Avoid catching colds, especially in the spring and autumn.
- Lead a regular life. Do not over work and avoid injuries. Make sure to get enough rest.
- Avoid mental excitement.
- Exercise regularly to build up the body's constitution and enhance the immune function. If you have herpes zoster, do not come into contact with children and pregnant women who can be very susceptible to disease.
- Keep the skin lesions clean to prevent secondary infections.
- Do not delay seeking medical attention, especially if the disease occurs on the head.
- Keep the bowels open so as to eliminate toxins.

Exercise – Qi Gong, Tai Ji

Since the occurrence of herpes zoster is rooted in a weakened immune system, prevention and daily care should pivot on enhancing body resistance. Qi gong and tai ji are two kinds of traditional exercises that can boost the body's constitution.

1. Tai Ji Quan 太极拳

Tai ji quan, a unique body-mind exercise, is a martial art based on Daoist philosophy and yin-yang theory. It is a special type of KungFu practiced to maintain health and for self-defense. Because it doesn't demand a lot of bodily energy or strength to learn, it is suitable for both young and old, and makes a great aerobic exercise. The more you practice, the better you will understand your own body, helping to coordinate and clear your body and mind. You will feel peace and physical, psychological, and emotional grace after practicing tai ji quan. Modern research has shown it to boost immunity, and it can help smooth stagnant qi and blood and improve the overall sense of well-being.

It is not clear when or where tai ji quan first began. There have been many schools of practice during its development over the past centuries. Presently the five major schools are Yang, Chen, Wu, Sun, and Wu. Whatever school you practice, you will be taught similar slow, graceful, smooth movements. The essence of tai ji quan is its harmonious natural movements; representing the constant transformation and interaction of yin and yang. Its movements are simple but subtle. It takes time, discipline and persistence to master the forms.

It is highly recommended that you learn tai ji from a qualified instructor. A DVD can help you get a rough idea about the basic movements and the sequence. But tai ji is not dancing or modeling, where the external form is most important; nor is it aerobics where the point is simply to get the heart rate going. You need an experienced instructor to guide you through the internal process as well as the external movements.

- Practice should be regular. Find a quiet place with fresh air. After you become familiar with the movements you will start to feel the subtle changes in your body.
- With a calm mind, guide your movements consciously, breathing slowly, deeply and naturally. Your movements should be stable, constant, gentle, and fluent. By learning to move slowly but consistently, your body can be trained to follow the subtle instructions of the brain. Gradually, coordination between your body and mind will be improved. A practitioner who had been learning tai ji for five years once fell down while riding a bicycle and to her surprise, she was not hurt at all. At the instant she fell down, her body naturally folded into the best position to avoid a head injury. This kind of ability to adjust to the environment is a higher level of vitality and leads to a greater state of health.
- Tai ji quan is both yin and yang, moving and still, hard and gentle, backward and forward, flexible and firm. Practicing tai ji can boost your qi and harmonize the yin and yang of your body. Practicing tai ji can make you feel refreshed, relaxed, and increase your awareness and enthusiasm for life. Tai ji is a door into the world of rediscovering your own body and how it relates to the world outside. It is for everyone.

There are no specially designed tai ji routines for the prevention of herpes zoster, but keeping to a general routine regularly is enough to strengthen the body and protect against disease. Studies have found that tai ji contributes to the prevention of herpes zoster. Dr. Irwin and his staff from the University of California at Los Angeles discovered tai ji was able to improve the bodily construction and enhance balance, but also help to prevent herpes zoster. Their research showed that tai ji increased immunity to herpes zoster[13].

2. Qi Gong 气功

Qi gong is divided into moving and still qi gong. Moving qi gong is practiced by coordinating body movements with breath and mind. Static qi gong focuses mostly on control and coordination of breath and mind, which is more difficult for beginners. Moving qi gong, which is often mistaken for tai ji, is what most people have seen before. Qi gong is not magic, nor is it mere exercise. For centuries it has been an important element of Chinese medicine. During the Spring and Autumn period (770-476 BC) or Warring States era (475-221 BC), a monograph on qi gong entitled *Inscription on Moving Qi on a Jade Pendant* (*Xíng Qì Yù Pèi Míng*) appeared. This text, possibly over 2,500 years old, was the first written reference to qi gong.

From the perspective of Chinese medical theory and practice, qi gong can supplement qi, strengthen the body, harmonize yin and yang, regulate qi and blood, smooth the flow in the channels, and calm down the mind.

However, it is more difficult to locate a real qi gong practitioner than to find a tai ji practitioner because qi gong is not easy to learn, practice, or evaluate. Scientists are still

exploring specific methods to study qi gong and some are showing prospects.

The key to practicing qi gong is the regulation and coordination of body, mind, and breath. You also must choose a style suitable for your condition. In most cases you will need an instructor.

Obsessive practicing may do more harm than good. A practice meant to relax the body and mind must be performed in a relaxed manner.

3. Research

- A group of 39 adults with at least one cardiovascular risk factor (hypertension, high cholesterol, smoking habit, or diabetes) joined a tai ji quan class for one hour three times a week for twelve weeks. The purpose of this study was to determine if tai ji could improve balance, muscle strength, endurance, and flexibility. At the beginning of the study all the patients fell below the 50th percentile of fitness in their age and gender groups. Improvement in all categories was evident after six weeks and further improvement after twelve, leading to the conclusion that tai ji practice could be of great benefit to the general health of the population[14].
- A study selected 5,159 men from England who were previously free from disease in order to determine the effect of physical activity on the incidence of heart disease and type II diabetes. After an average 17-year follow-up, the authors concluded that the risk of developing either of these diseases decreased with increasing amounts of physical activity[15]. Similar results were collected from the Finnish Diabetes Prevention Study[16] conducted in 2000.

Chapter 4

How Does Chinese Medicine Treat Herpes Zoster?

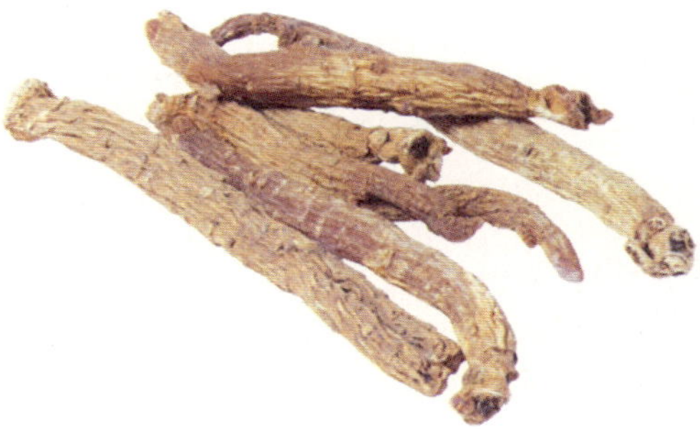

In the language of Chinese medicine, herpes zoster can be categorized into many patterns or types, the most frequent ones are as follows. They are:

- Excess fire of the liver and gallbladder channels
- Dampness and heat of the spleen and stomach
- Qi stagnation and blood stasis

Three Common Patterns of Herpes Zoster

Patterns	Symptoms and Signs	Treatement Principles
Excess fire of the liver and gallbladder channels	Clearly defined, deep red skin lesions and blisters with tense walls, distributed along the waist and rib side (liver and gallbladder channels), burning and stabbing pain, bitter taste in mouth, dry throat, fidgeting, irritability, constipation, scanty dark yellow urine, red tongue, yellow tongue coating, wiry rapid pulse.	Clear heat and purge fire, remove toxins and relieve pain
Dampness and heat of the spleen and stomach	Pale red skin lesions with loose blister walls that are easily split and often filled with pus, mostly on the abdomen and lower limbs, numbness or burning pain, a greasy feeling in the mouth, thirst without a strong desire to drink, poor appetite, bloating after meals, soft stool or difficult bowel movements, greasy tongue coating, slippery and rapid pulse.	Strengthen the spleen and drain damp, clear heat and remove toxins
Qi stagnation and blood stasis	Blisters with purple-red color, possibly blood filled, or later stage lesions that have scabbed or scarred over, stabbing pain, listlessness, difficulty sleeping, fidgeting, dark purplish tongue, white tongue coating, wiry pulse.	Promote qi flow, remove blood stasis, dredge the liver and relieve pain

The process of pattern differentiation is a highly intellectual, innovative, and individualized practice. Although in recent years, biomedicine has tried to achieve individualized treatment, it is fulfilled and practiced to the maximum extent in Chinese medicine. When faced with different patients with the same disease, the Chinese medical practitioner will offer sometimes quite different prescriptions for each case. Pattern identification can only be accomplished by using sound judgment based on an interactive, humane interview between an experienced practitioner and a patient. The ability to do correct pattern identification is what defines a skilled doctor of Chinese medicine.

Herbal Decoction

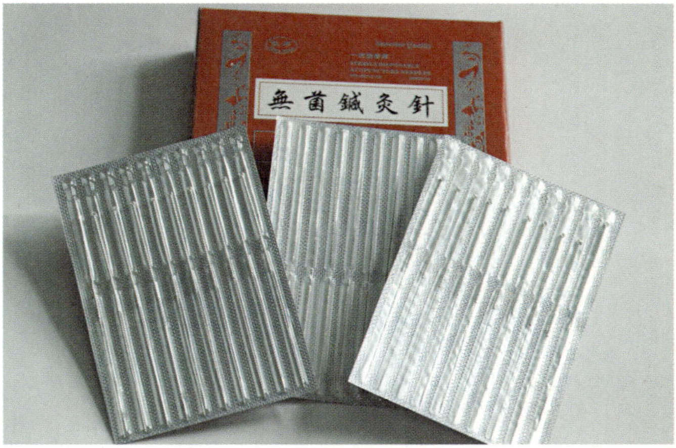

Acupuncture Needles

Using pattern identification, treatment methods often vary. Herbal medication is the first choice in the management of herpes zoster and is administered orally or sometimes applied topically. Non-herbal medication includes acupuncture, moxibustion, massage, etc. The exact program will consist of a detailed selection of herbs, their dosage and method of administration, and an acupuncture point selection, manipulation techniques, and duration of treatment, all of which are based on the individual patient's pattern. Several methods can be combined for the same patient to ensure comprehensive treatment.

The use of modern biomedicine integrated with Chinese medicine has increased the scope of treatment available. With the help of modern technology, Chinese medicine has a better understanding of herpes zoster thanks to laboratory tests and biomedical diagnostic guidelines. Pattern identification becomes more accurate without losing its advantage of promoting the ability of human body to heal itself. Chinese medicine can provide numerous treatment methods for herpes zoster. The following sections will talk about the major ones.

Acupuncture and Moxibustion

1. What Is Acupuncture and Moxibustion?

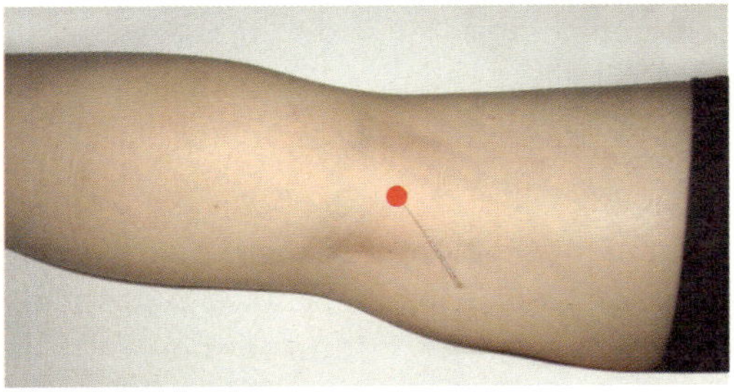

Wěi Zhōng (BL 40)

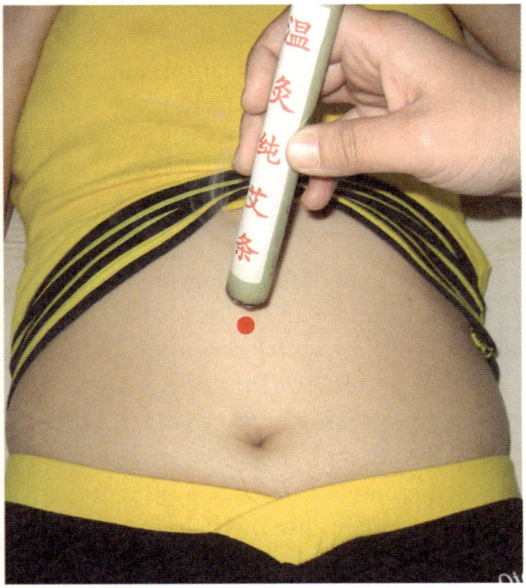

Shàng Wǎn (RN 13)

Zhen Jiu is the Chinese term that refers to acupuncture and moxibustion, the treatment methods that have been characteristic of Chinese medicine for thousands of years.

These days, acupuncture is everywhere. Searching online, one can read hundreds of reports of research involved in the scientific exploration of this ancient art. Acupuncture and moxibustion have been proven effective in various diseases from cardiology to psychology. One reason these techniques are so popular is that they are absolutely safe when properly administered by a trained acupuncturist, even though the thought of being needled can be unsettling to many first time patients. For most people in the west, it is difficult to understand how a fine needle inserted into the foot can relieve a headache, why a fetus's position can be reversed by needling a toe, or how puncturing a spot on the wrist can help insomnia. All of these actions are easily explained in the language of Chinese medicine, but there are still many theories on what exactly is at work in modern scientific terms.

As biomedicine has no specific remedy for herpes zoster, and fails to effectively relieve the pain, acupuncture and moxibustion can make up for these shortcomings. Acupuncture can eliminate the blisters and redness, ward off postherpetic neuralgia, and shorten the length of the illness, all this with no side effects. Usually obvious improvement is evident after 1-3 treatments, perhaps slightly longer for postherpetic neuralgia.

In order to understand acupuncture, moxibustion, or channel theory, an understanding of Chinese medical theory is necessary.

Channels & collaterals (*Jīng luò*)

In the theory of Chinese medicine, the human body is an organic whole and the internal organs, external surface, and extremities are connected to each other by a network called the *jīng luò* (channels & collaterals). According to this theory, the channels and collaterals connect the internal organs with the external surface and extremities by transporting qi and blood. Analogy can

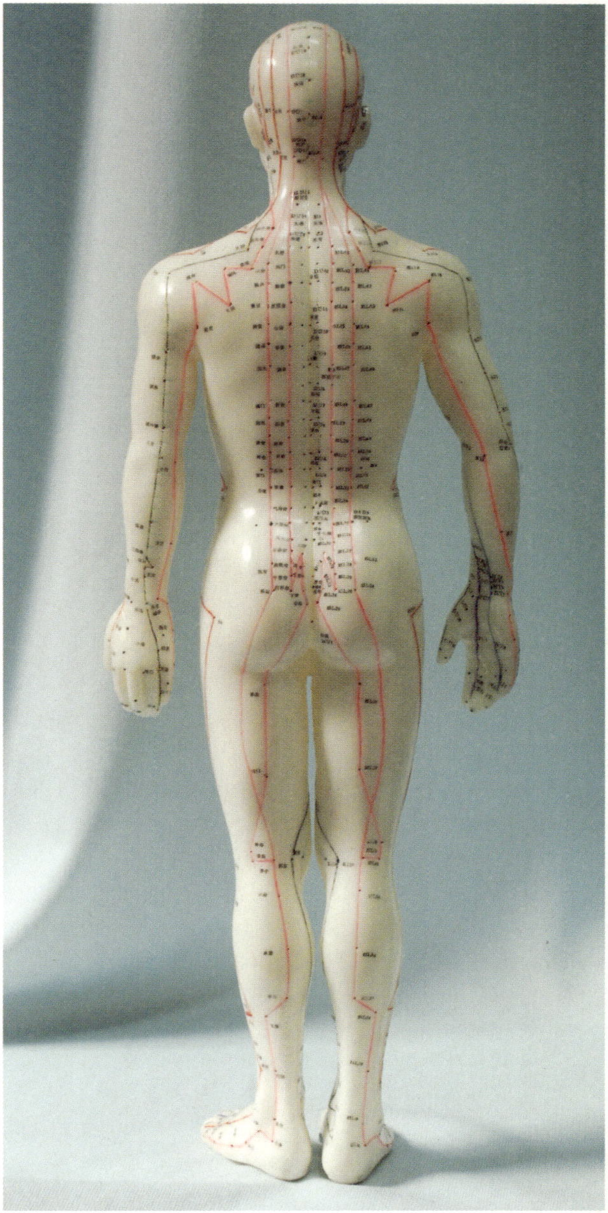

Channels on the Back

be made between this network and the earth's water system. With big rivers as the main thoroughfares, and the tributaries as smaller branches, the whole planet is closely connected. Acupuncture and moxibustion are applied according to this system. By stimulating the points (*xué wèi*, 穴位), or the gates of this network, the human body will be influenced, moving naturally towards healing. Acupuncture points are the openings of these channels and collaterals. Inserting needles into these points will stimulate or block the flow of qi and blood. When properly administered, the flow of qi and blood will be smoothed and organ functions will be restored. Weakness is strengthened while excess is reduced. Therefore balance is restored and health is regained.

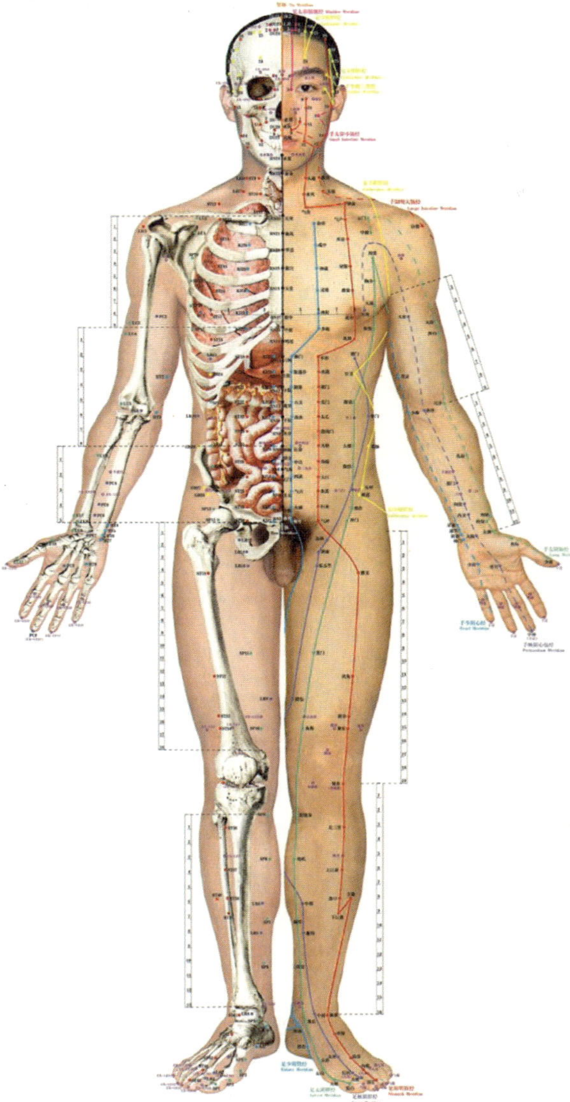

2. How Does Acupuncture Work?

The underlying mechanism is still being researched. There exist many theories as to how acupuncture may affect the human body, and each one can explain part of the picture. In studies of its pain-relieving effect, researchers found that acupuncture blocks the impulse transmissions between the spinal cord and brain, stopping pain by closing the nerve fibers that carry impulses. This is a common theory and often referred to as the gate control theory. Various other theories also attempt to answer the question from different angles. The theory of boosting immunity states that levels of important substances such as white blood cells, antibodies, triglycerides, and gamma blovulins are raised during treatment and this stimulates the immune response. Another theory states that endorphins, which act to both stop pain and promote a sense of well-being, are stimulated through acupuncture. Neurotransmitter studies show that levels of seratonin and noradrenaline are altered during treatment. The circulatory theory involves the release of vasodilators, which cause blood vessels to constrict and dilate.

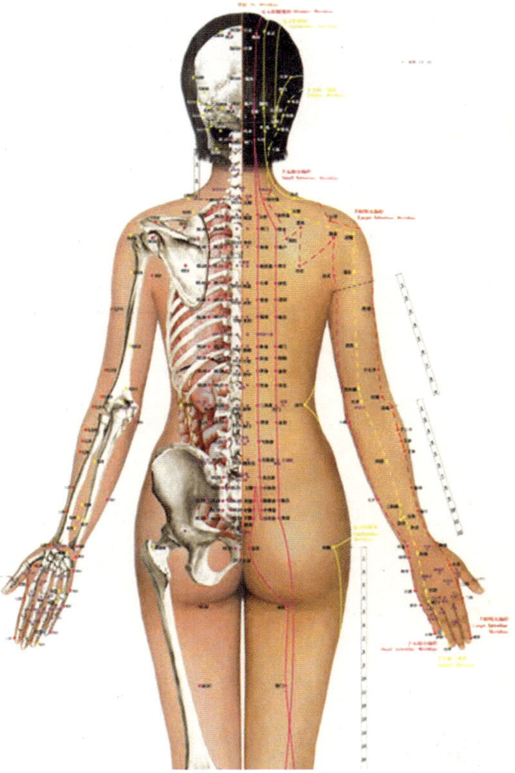

What we can conclude from these theories is that acupuncture acts on many targets. A synthesized drug has a definite target and expected effects together with expected side-effects as well. The function of acupuncture is done in reverse, by stimulating the body's power to regulate its own function and relieving localized symptoms. The relief of symptoms are only 'side-effects' of the general changes going on at the root level.

Acupuncture needles

The most common acupuncture needles are called filiform needles, which are normally between 0.5 to 1.5 inches long (1.5 - 4.5 cm), but can be up to 5 inches (15cm) depending on the location of the point to be needled and the size of the patient. The needles are usually made of stainless steel, but gold and silver needles are sometimes used. The needles are used on one patient and then disposed of in a medical 'sharps' container.

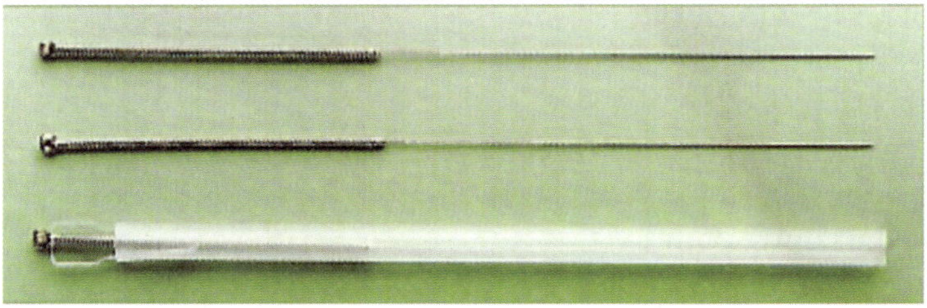

Acupuncture positions

Different positions are used based on the points selected. As long as the patient feels comfortable, any position is suitable. Common positions are as shown in the pictures:

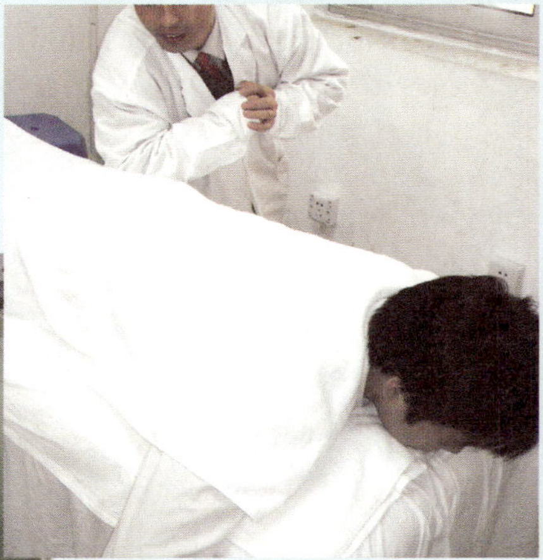

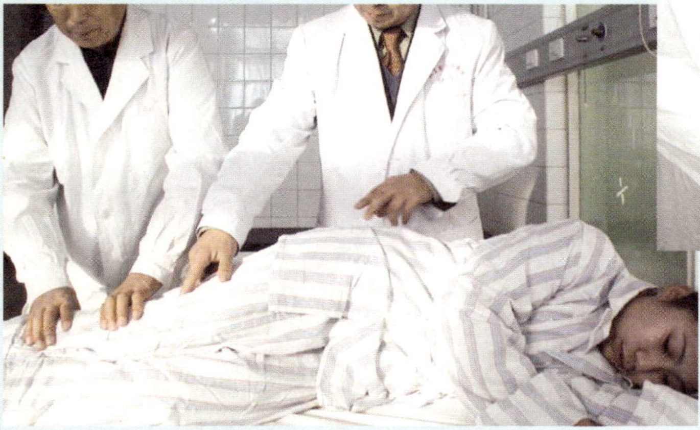

Clean needling practice

Acupuncturists are required to take a course called the "Clean Needle Technique" to train them how to handle, insert, and remove needles so both patient and practitioner are protected from any kind of contamination. The acupuncturist will wash his or her hands thoroughly with soap and water before and after treatment, and the points to be needled will be disinfected by swabbing the point with a cotton swab dipped in 75% alcohol. Anything that punctures the skin will be sterile, and any other implements used will be thoroughly sanitized between patients.

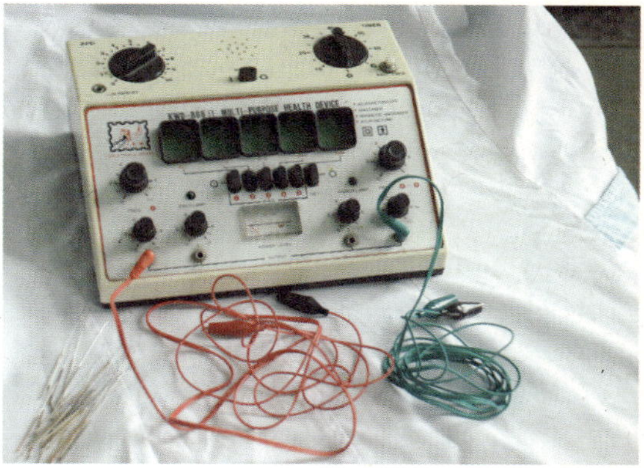

Electroacupuncture Apparatus

Electroacupuncture

Currently, it is common for practitioners to choose to use an electrical apparatus that allows an electrical impulse to be sent through the acupuncture needles to mimic constant manipulation. Practitioners are trained to operate the machines in the safest way and the amount of power sent through the needles is usually only a few microamperes. Electroacupuncture is commonly used for problems that require constant needle stimulation. The machine will allow the practitioner to do other work while the point is receiving stimulation. Originating from China, this technique is commonly used in many countries. The frequency and the amount of power used in electroacupuncture tend to vary to a great degree depending on the patient's condition and the practitioner's decision.

Commonly used acupuncture points

There are hundreds of points on the human body, most of which are situated along fourteen main channels. Some of the points are more commonly used than others. The points selected in the management of herpes zoster can vary greatly, according to the patterns, the patient, and the practitioner's experience. The final prescription of point selection depends on your specific condition and the practitioner's judgment.

The action of every point is to regulate yin and yang, the difference is in what exact way each point works. Some points work on the qi aspect, while others may work on the blood; some are warming, and others are cooling. Most point functions have not been verified by modern research, but for some of the more important points, some research has been done.

Below are some photos and descriptions of commonly used points in the management of herpes zoster. Of course all patients are different, so not everyone will get all of these points. But since these are major points, everyone is likely to experience at least a couple of these points during the course of treatment.

Qū chí (Large Intestine 11)

Qū chí is an important point on the large intestine channel. The large intestine is the exhaust pipe of the body and heat and dampness can be purged through the stool. *Qū chí* is used for clearing heat of the whole body and excels at managing skin problems.

The name means "Pool at the Bend" and refers to both the function and the location. It invokes an image of water that can clear away heat and toxins. The location is on the outside of the arm just above the elbow.

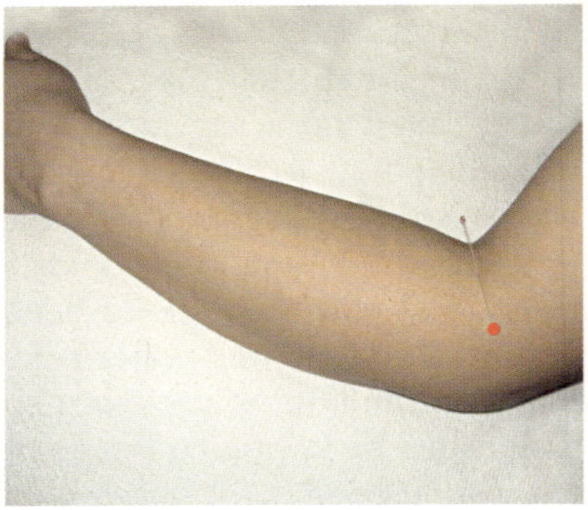

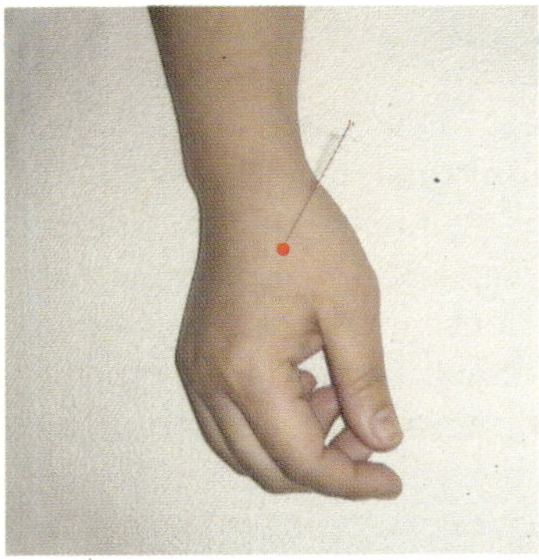

Hé gŭ (Large Intestine 4)

Hé gŭ, also on the large intestine channel, is the source point of this channel. This is an important point to clear heat and move stagnation in the body.

Hé gŭ is located on the skin between the thumb and index finger.

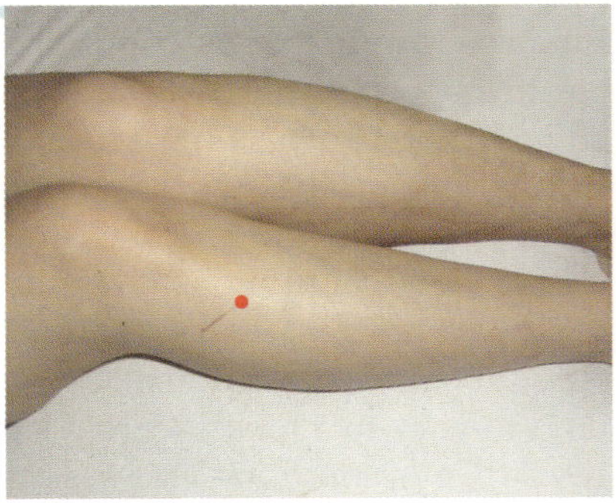

Zú sān lĭ (Stomach 36)

Arguably the most important point on the body, *zú sān lĭ* , which means "leg three mile", is the primary point used when the body's qi is weak. The name informs the practitioner that needling here will help the patient walk three more miles on their life journey. It is located on the stomach channel and can be used for any digestive disorder. Since the body's qi is largely produced by the digestive system, the importance of good digestion to health cannot be exaggerated. It is useful in treating dampness, strengthening body resistance, regulating qi and promoting healthy skin.

Zú sān lĭ is located roughly one hands breadth (4 fingers) from the bottom of the knee cap, on the outside of the leg. It is often somewhat sensitive when pressed.

Yīn líng quán (Spleen 9)

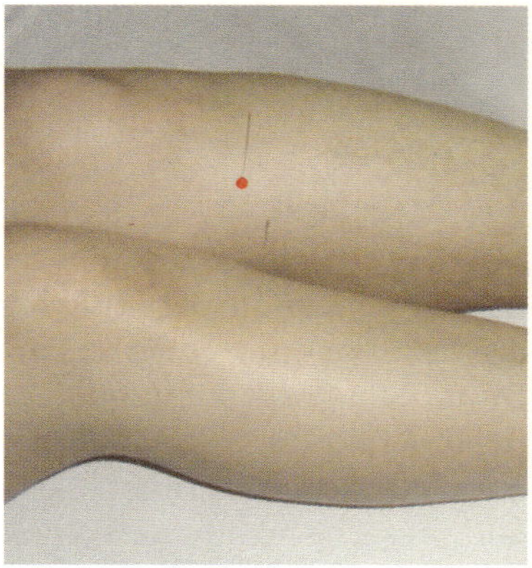

Yīn líng quán is on the spleen channel. The spleen is in charge of digestion and fluid metabolism. This point excels at removing pathogenic fluid (dampness) and strengthening the spleen so it can function better. In addition to damp types of herpes zoster, this point is often used in diseases such as edema, jaundice, diarrhea and urinary problems. It works by strengthening the spleen to remove the damp.

Yīn líng quán is located on the inner side of the leg, up towards the knee just below the bony knob.

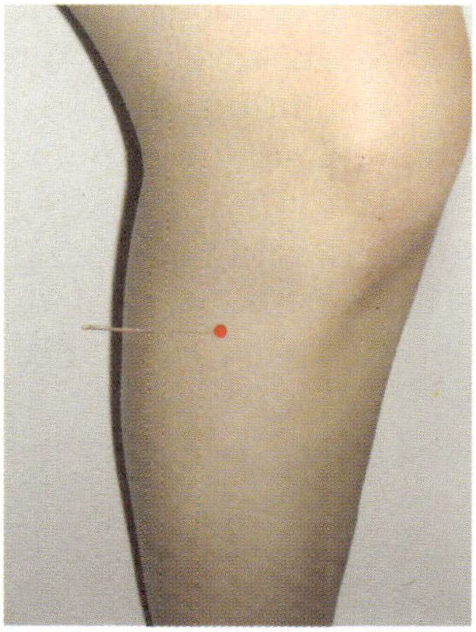

Yáng líng quán (Gallbladder 34)

Yáng líng quán is on the gallbladder channel and is a gathering point of qi on this channel. Because herpes zoster is usually distributed along the liver and gallbladder channels, this point is often selected to move stagnation and clear heat in these channels. As opposed to the similarly named *yīn líng quán*, this point works by activating the channels and removing stagnation and heat.

Yáng líng quán is located opposite to *yīn líng quán* on the outer side of the leg, below the bony knobs of the knee.

A shi points

A shi points, literally translated as, "Ah, that's it!" are not regular acupuncture channel points. There are places on your body that when pressed, you will say "Ah, that's it!" meaning that the point pressed is where the pain is. Since sensitive points can appear anywhere in the body, these points have no specific names. In herpes zoster they are usually located in the region where the lesions are concentrated, though sometimes they can be found in distant areas.

In clinical practice, acupuncture is usually combined with other techniques to manage herpes zoster.

Moxibustion

Moxibustion is the application of heat using a small bundle of tightly bound herbs that are burnt over targeted acupuncture points. By applying heat stimulation to certain points the practitioner can regulate the yin-yang balance of the internal organs to prevent disease and preserve health. Based on the same theories as acupuncture, it is another type of external treatment method. The material used in moxibustion is usually made of artemisia leaves, commonly called mugwort. The Chinese herbal medical classic *Miscellaneous Records of Famous Physicians (Míng Yī Bié Lù)* based on the legendary *Divine Husbandman's Classic of the Materia Medica (Shén Nóng Běn Cǎo Jīng)*, states that artemisia leaves are bitter, slightly warm, without any toxicity, and should be used in moxibustion to manage all types of disease. Artemisia leaves, warm in nature, can promote the flow of qi and blood, remove dampness and cold, and dissolve masses and accumulations in order to cure illness, prevent disease and maintain health. Moxibustion has been used for thousands of years, longer even than stone needles, the ancient precursors to modern acupuncture needles. Like acupuncture, much research has been done on the effects of moxibustion on the body. Presently, it is widely used as an effective supplement for acupuncture.

In the language of Chinese medicine, the major actions of moxibustion are to regulate yin and yang by supplementing yang, improve the circulation of qi and blood in the channels, help the body to fight invading pathogens, supplement qi and blood, and regulate the internal organs. These functions illustrate how moxibustion can prevent disease and delay aging.

Moxibustion is often used to manage the pain associated with herpes zoster. The heat stimulates the qi and blood in the channels to remove stagnation and relieve pain.

Mugwort

Moxa Poles

Moxa Cones

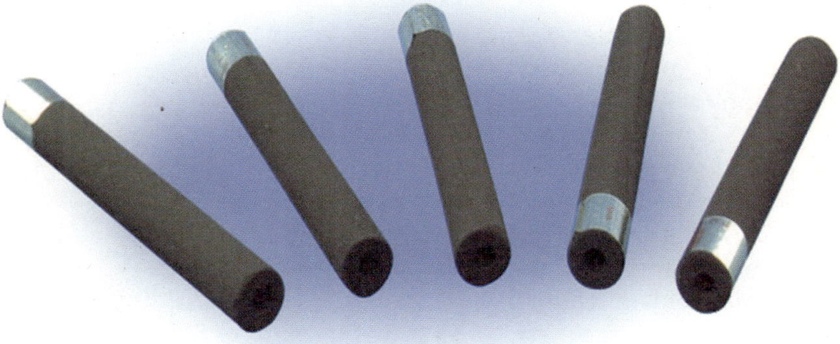
Moxa Pole

Types of moxibustion

Direct moxibustion

Direct moxibustion uses what are called moxa cones. These are usually shaped to roughly half an inch (1.5cm) high, placed directly on acupuncture points, lit, and left in place until the cone is burnt out or until the sensation becomes painful. This is a strong form of treatment and can produce pain, blisters, and even scarring. Some Chinese traditions still deliberately induce scarring, which is believed to have the strongest effect. This method is usually reserved for serious cases being treated by experienced practitioners.

Indirect moxibustion

The second, more common form of moxibustion is indirect moxibustion. It involves either the use a cigar-shaped moxa pole, or the burning of moxa cones on top of a layer of ginger, garlic, or salt. With a moxa

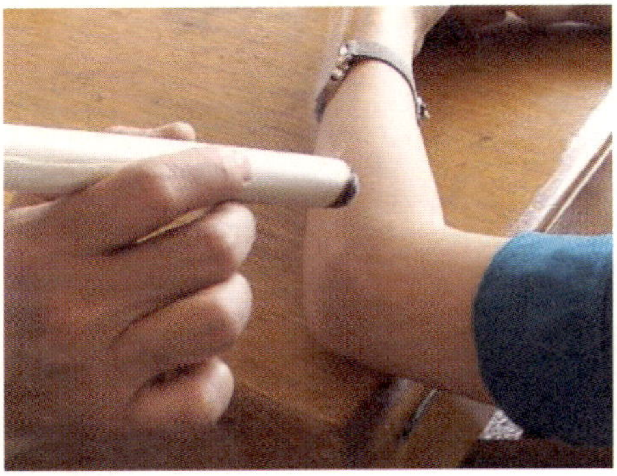

pole, a practitioner holds the stick roughly 1.5 inches (4.5cm) above the skin and holds it in place until the skin becomes red or appears congested. When garlic, ginger, or salt is used with moxibustion, they provide a buffer from the heat of the moxa as well as adding their own properties to the therapeutic effect. These forms of treatment do not usually cause severe pain or leave any blisters or scars, though the skin may remain red for a while.

For people who have asthma or other respiratory problems, smokeless moxa can be used.

Practitioners also sometimes place the moxa cone on top of an acupuncture needle and burn it. If good ventilation is not available, heat can also be applied to points from an electrical source designed for the purpose as well.

Moxibustion is not for everyone. It is indicated mainly for patients suffering from cold, dampness, or stagnation. It is not used regularly on anyone diagnosed with too much heat. But if there are isolated problems such as pain, injury, or digestive problems, moxa may be used. However, moxa can be used to manage herpes zoster due to heat as long as the course is short.

Ear acupuncture

Placing needles in the ear is a new addition to Chinese medicine's treatment arsenal. Similar to reflexology, the ear represents a microsystem of the entire body. The shape of the ear is described by ear

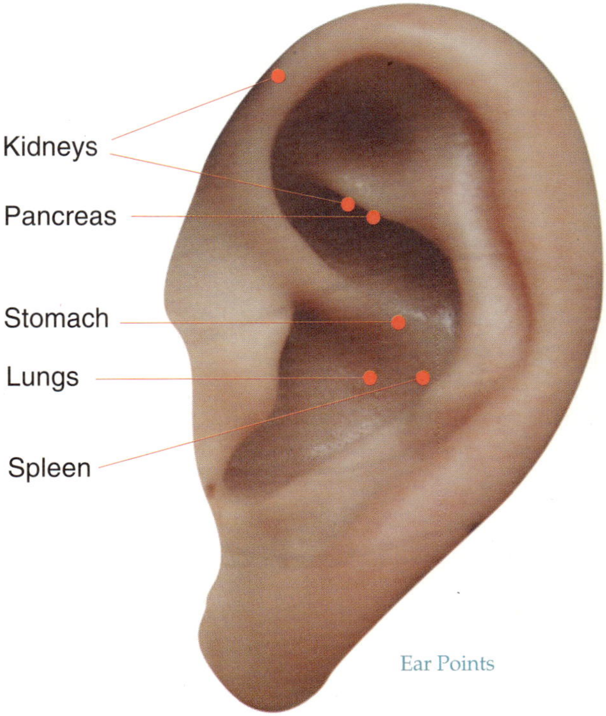

Ear Points

specialists as looking like a curled up human figure upside down, with the head as the lobe and the legs curled up to form the top of the ear. The entire human body with all its different parts and organs has been mapped out. Although there are specialists who mainly use ear acupuncture, most practitioners use it as a helpful adjunct therapy. A popular technique is to place a small seed, metal pellet, or tiny needle on an ear point and keep it in place with a small piece of tape. These objects will then provide a constant stimulation to the points chosen. Usually you will be instructed to press or rub each of these points several times a day for a few minutes. This convenient form of therapy allows for around the clock treatment. Normally the tape can be taken off in three or four days.

Other techniques

Though acupuncture and moxibustion are the main techniques used by practitioners of Chinese medicine, there are a variety of other techniques that may be used. These include but are not limited to cupping, *gua sha*, plum-blossom needling, dermal needling, and burning-rush moxibustion. These techniques may cause slight damage to the skin and tissues, but in turn, they stimulate the points much more strongly and the effect lasts longer. If applied properly, these techniques can sometimes be more effective than conventional acupuncture for pain relief. As for herpes zoster, these techniques can either be applied alone or be used in combination. For example, cupping is often combined with dermal needling. The technique involves inducing redness and slight bleeding by tapping with a dermal needle and then applying cups over the areas to draw out the stagnation and heat[17].

Cimicfuga

Cupping

Cupping involves the application of suctions cups to the skin either near the painful area or on a related channel. Air is removed from the cups by using a burning cotton ball soaked in alcohol (modern cups using air suction are also used). There is usually no pain involved in cupping, though the sensation of suction is sometimes strange the first time.

Plum-Blossom Needle

A small hammer with several small needles is used to stimulate the skin and remove stagnation. The tapping is very light, but because of the needles the sensation is a little sharp, though not intense. Small drops of blood sometimes emerge from the area being tapped, helping to remove stagnation and heat.

Cupping

Plum-blossom Needle

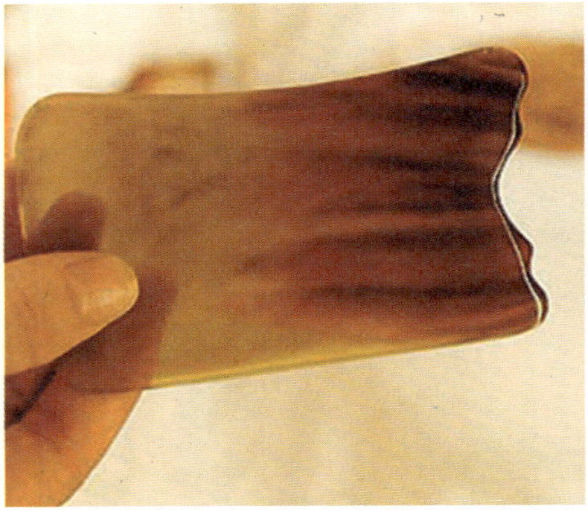

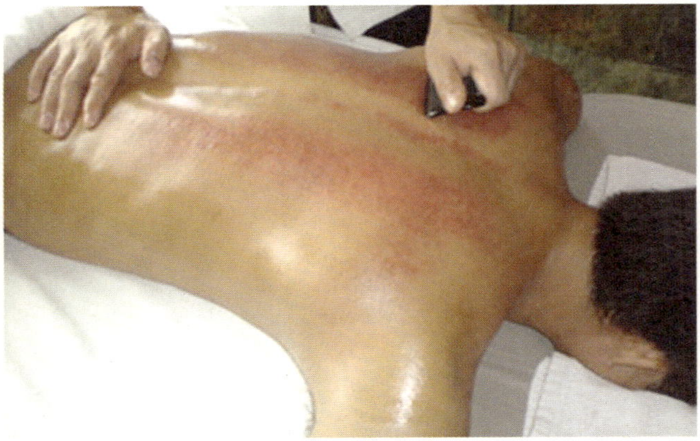

Gua Sha

Gua Sha

Gua sha is technique of rubbing the skin and is used in many cultures. It is usually used for pain that hasn't had time to go very deep. The rapid, light scraping techniques are not painful, but will elicit slight bruising in the area. These bruises are very superficial and not painful and are a sign that the congestion causing pain has been activated and is leaving the body.

Case 4

Mr. Zhang, a 31 year old male, came for treatment with Chinese medicine. He presented with two dense areas of lesions in his right upper abdomen. The lesions were roughly the size of small grains of rice and located on the path of a spinal nerve like a belt around the waist. He complained of uneasiness in the skin and the pain was seriously aggravated if he put on clothes. This was a typical case of herpes zoster. The physician selected *a shi* points in the region as the chief points. After making sure the area was clean, a three-edged needle was used to prick the areas surrounding the lesions and a small amount of blood was allowed to come out. After this treatment a moxa pole was used for about 20 minutes. Finally, conventional acupuncture was used on the point *yáng líng quán* (GB 34) with twirling manipulation. This same treatment was given once a day. After three days, the patient was happy because his herpes zoster was totally cured[18].

Cautions and contraindications for treatment with acupuncture and moxibustion

Acupuncture and its adjunct modalities are an incredibly safe kind of therapy. However, there are certain times when great care must be taken and even times when treatment should not be administered or when the equipment is not available for treatment. Fortunately for the patient, the scope of techniques available to the practitioner of Chinese medicine is very wide. If one treatment avenue is blocked, there will probably be another that is open and available. Patients with herpes zoster should be especially careful to keep the lesions clean as patients with this disease are vulnerable to infections.

The following are some other cautions and contraindications for treatment with acupuncture, moxibustion, or other techniques.

- Any acute metabolic disorder is contraindicated for acupuncture and moxibustion.
- Extreme hunger, fatigue and mental stress are not indicated for acupuncture and moxibustion.
- Pregnant women can be treated, but the practitioner must be very cautious.
- History of fainting during acupuncture treatments.
- Acupuncture and moxibustion treatment must go together with dietary restriction and life style management.

3. What Will My Treatment Program Be Like?

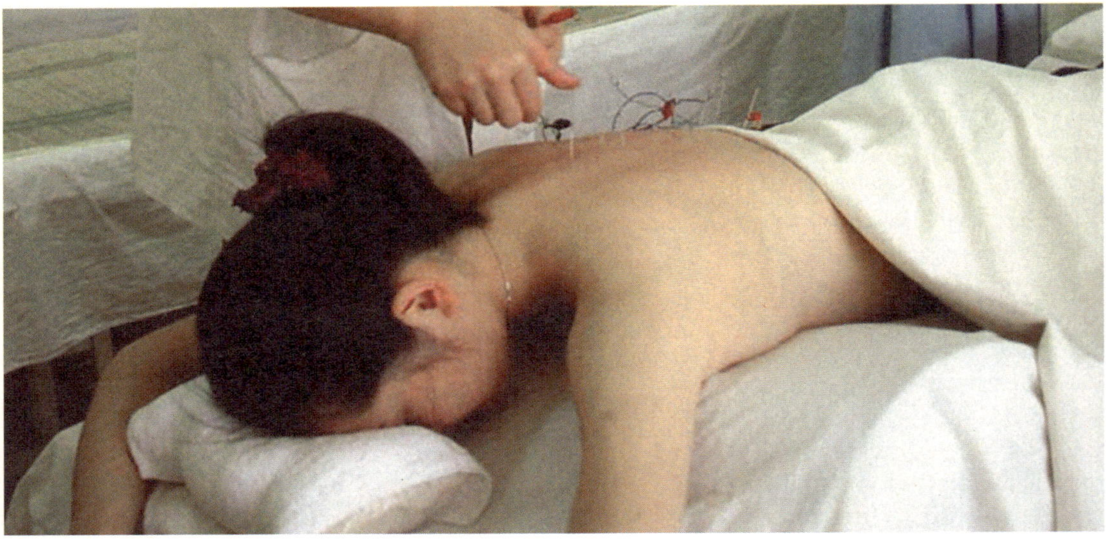

After collecting detailed information (symptoms, signs, environment, tongue inspection, and pulse taking) the Chinese medical practitioner will identify the pattern of disharmonies present. Based on this pattern identification, an optimal treatment protocol will be drawn up according to theories of Chinese medicine.

The practitioner will then decide which modality (needles, moxa, cupping, etc.) to use during the present treatment. Usually needling is performed and often one or more additional treatment modalities are used. The number and location of the needles is decided by the acupuncturist and will probably vary from treatment to treatment, though some points will remain the same and begin to feel familiar. The points that remain the same are usually for your underlying root condition, while the points that change frequently are often to deal with whatever symptoms are most serious at the time of treatment. The amount of needles is not set and can be as few as two or three or as many as thirty, but usually is around ten to fifteen. Needles are mainly placed on the abdomen, back and limbs, with points on the scalp and face also used from time to time. The depth of the needles is determined by the specific points since the amount of flesh is different throughout the body. The length of needles is also decided by the acupuncturist and normally is between 0.5 and 1.5 inches (1.5 - 4.5cm).

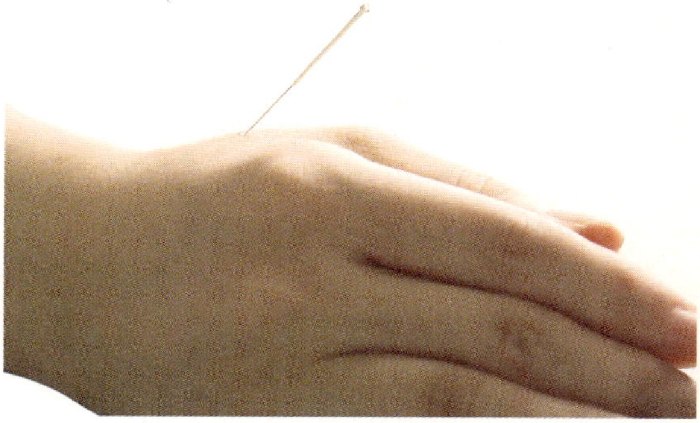

What can I expect during an acupuncture treatment?

The needles are inserted quickly at an angle of 15 to 90 degrees in relation to the skin's surface. When an experienced acupuncturist inserts the needles, there is not usually any pain. The sensation is at most like being bitten by an ant. Acupuncture needles are much finer than the hypodermic needles used in hospitals. But most importantly, trained acupuncturists can insert the needles quickly and correctly without causing unnecessary discomfort.

Once the needle has been inserted there are a variety of techniques like raising, thrusting, twirling, plucking and scraping, which strengthen the stimulation and sensation. The technique used will depend on the disease that is being managed. The patient is supposed to get a specific sensation called *"de qi"*. *De qi* is a sensation specific to acupuncture and literally means "obtaining the qi". The exact feeling varies with each individual patient. It is usually not pain but a unique sensation of soreness, heaviness, distension, or radiation in some direction. It is generally believed that the stronger the *de qi* sensation is, the more effective the acupuncture will be. After a few treatments, patients usually start to enjoy this sensation because it is both pleasant and they know the good results it brings.

During treatment, it is best to relax and move as little as possible, unless the practitioner asks you to. Too much movement might cause the needles to bend, get stuck, or even break. These accidents are very rare, but if anything happens, stay calm and let the practitioner remove the needles immediately.

After the needles are inserted, the patient is usually left to relax for about 20-40 minutes. Other techniques such as moxa or cupping can be performed before or after needling, depending on the practitioner. After the needles are removed, get up slowly and carefully. There is normally no bleeding during or after acupuncture treatment. If bleeding occurs, it will only

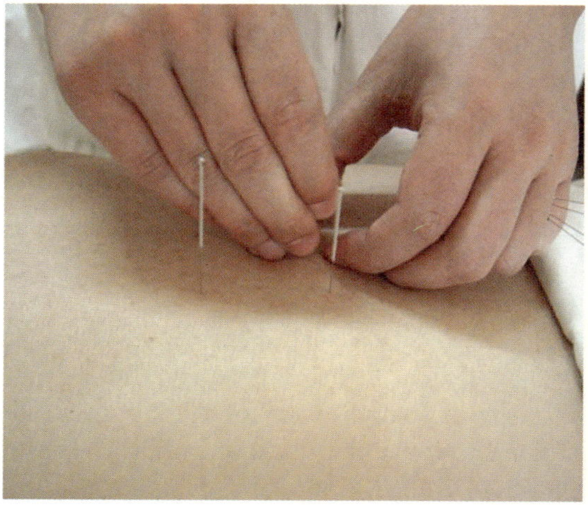

be a few drops due to the breakage of small capillaries. Bruising is also very rare, but sometimes happens due to subcutaneous bleeding also from broken capillaries.

After treatment, you will probably feel relaxed and energized. Some of your symptoms may disappear instantly. You may sleep better, have a more regulated appetite, feel less pain, or experience less anxiety.

In rare cases a patient will be over responsive to treatment. This usually occurs when a patient is extremely hungry, weak, nervous, or the stimulation and *de qi* sensation is too strong. The patient might experience nausea, possibly vomiting, develop a very pale complexion, feel weak, sweat excessively, or even faint. If this happens, the acupuncturist will remove all the needles and allow the patient to lie down and rest for a while. Normally the patient will recover quickly. If the patient still feels unwell, a few points may be needled that will help relieve the patient's symptoms.

It is advised to be in the best condition possible when you have acupuncture. Don't come for acupuncture when you are very hungry or just after a big meal, and try to be rested. Get the most out of your treatment by being extra careful of your general health the day before and after treatment. Help Chinese medicine help you!

A typical treatment course for herpes zoster will be once every other day for about seven days. After this, the practitioner and patient will reevaluate and decide on future treatment. Since herpes zoster is an acute disease, treatment will take no more than a month. For those with post-herpetic neuralgia, treatment will be somewhat longer, but results should be felt within a week or two of starting therapy.

Even though most patients begin to feel some relief after the first several treatments, acupuncture is working on a very deep level and to effect lasting change, ample time must be given. The journey to health with Chinese medicine is like everything else in the natural world, there will be ups and downs, times of rapid growth and times of hibernation. With commitment and good communication between practitioner and patient, the journey can be life changing.

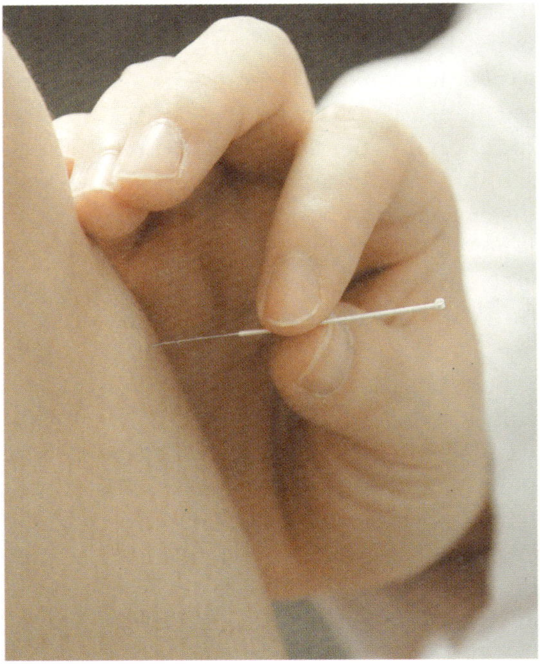

4. Translated Research

Over the past half century, the Chinese government has given a lot of support to the practice and study of its traditional medicine. Due to this support, thousands of clinical trials and research projects have been performed on the effect of acupuncture, Chinese medicinals, moxibustion, qi gong, and other modalities on different diseases. There is a wealth of scientific information that is largely unavailable in English. Below, and in the following chapters, we have summarized the results of some of the studies performed on patients with herpes zoster to show that not only are the results of Chinese medicine noticeable to the patient, but can be recorded by modern scientific techniques as well.

- Wang Shan-sheng et al. used plum-blossom needling to treat 192 patients with herpes zoster. The technique was to tap frequently along the normal skin around the herpes lesions with medium strength until there was a slight bloody exudate. This treatment was given once a day. 166 cases were cured within 3 days, while the others took from 4 to 10 days[19].

- Yan Li et al. treated patients by needling *jiá jǐ* (EX-B2) points on the affected side. As long as the needling sensation radiated to rib cage region, the needles were retained for up to 15-20 minutes. Then, a three-edged needle was applied to prick the skin around the herpes lesions and cupping was applied over the pricked areas. Among 18 patients treated by this therapy 17 were cured in 1-6 treatments and 1 was improving[20].

- Liu Yuan-ba et al. chose different points to treat herpes zoster occurring in different regions. For herpes in the face, he selected *hé gǔ* (LI 4); on the top of head, *liè quē* (LU 7); in regions of chest and hypochondrium, *nèi guān* (PC 6); in the abdomen, *zú sān lǐ* (ST 36); lesser abdomen, *sān yīn jiāo* (SP 6); lumbar and back, *wěi zhōng* (BL 40); hip, *huán tiào* (GB 30); and the four limbs, *yáng líng quán* (GB 34). After point selection, he applied moxibustion, treating once a day. 52 patients were treated by this method and they were all cured within 6 days. Generally, the pain disappeared within 4 days and the herpes scabbed over in 2 to 5 days[21].

● Tian Mao et al. held that herpes zoster was caused by heat stagnation in numerous organs, saturating in the muscles and skin. It frequently occurs in the chest, rib side, and back, along the course of the liver, spleen, and bladder channels. They applied plum-blossom needling to prick the border of the herpes lesions from the lower borders upwards. *Jiá jǐ* (EX-B2) points on the back and points of the bladder channel were pricked as well. At the same time, body acupuncture was given. The chief points selected were *qū chí* (LI 11), *hé gǔ* (LI 4), and *a shi* points. After needling, the needles were retained for 30 minutes and treatment given once a day. As a result, 85 cases in the study were all cured[22].

● Cai Rong et al. used moxibustion to treat 203 cases of herpes zoster. This involved the use of a moxa pole above the lesions, held in place until the skin changed to a deep red or turned from translucent to milky white. Treatment was given 3 times a day for 5 days. As a result, 176 cases were cured, 27 cases showed improvement, thus showing an effective rate of 100 percent[23].

● Wang Yan et al. used a three-edged needle to treat herpes zoster by pricking the border of the skin lesions and then cupping over the area. The cups were retained for 10-15 minutes. Body acupuncture was also used on *yáng líng quán* (GB 34) and *yīn líng quán* (SP 9). This therapy was given once a day for 10 days. Among 130 patients managed by this therapy, 107 cases were cured, 21 cases showed significant improvement, and 27 cases had some kind of effect[24].

● Huang Yu-xi et al. applied a needle pricking method to the two ends and the middle of the belt-shaped zone of lesions. Immediately after pricking, he used cupping and retained the cups for 5-10 minutes. Among 67 patients treated by this therapy, 64 cases were cured in 1 to 3 treatments, and 3 cases had some effect[25].

● Ren Xiu-lan et al. used a plum-blossom needle to tap the skin around the lesions until there was slight bleeding. Cupping was applied immediately after the tapping. 37 patients were treated by this therapy, and all were cured with just one treatment[26].

Chinese Medicinals

1. What Are Chinese Medicinals?

Introduction

The phrase 'Chinese Medicinal' refers to substances that occur naturally in the environment and can come from plant, animal, or mineral sources. These substances can be prepared in a variety of ways so that they can be used by the body. Chinese medicinals can be drunk, eaten, inhaled, or applied to the skin. They can regulate the body's qi, blood, yin, yang, and expel pathogens as well. There are over 3,000 different substances listed in ancient pharmacology books, though only about 400 or so are commonly used. In fact, any natural substance can be used in Chinese medicine, but it will be called a Chinese medicinal only when it is used according to the theories of Chinese medicine.

In skin disorders such as herpes zoster, Chinese medicinals can be used to relieve symptoms, manage the course, and improve the patient's quality of life.

Traditional Medicinal Chest

Mechanism of Chinese Medicinals

The underlying idea between how Chinese medicinals work is fundamentally different than that behind biomedical pharmaceuticals. A pharmaceutical is a finely crafted and intensely focused creation. Years, sometimes decades, of research goes before any drug is released on the market. Scientists strive to isolate the exact chemical or combination of chemicals that can cause a very specific change in bodily function. The change elicited by these drugs is often effective at relieving symptoms, but does not usually restore the damaged body part or function that was responsible for the symptoms in the first place. For example, antibiotics will kill invading bacteria, but will not strengthen the body against further invasions; or a pain killer may relieve the aching joints of an arthritis patient, but it will not stop or even retard the progression of the disease. In addition, it is not uncommon for a drug to cause unwanted side-effects in addition to its desired actions. Biomedical drugs may damage the nervous system, the digestive system, or most commonly the liver or kidneys.

In Chinese medicine, as mentioned above, the idea is to restore the body's innate ability to remain in a state of health. In severe cases, long-term treatment is necessary to provide constant support to the body, but usually patients who start treatment with Chinese medicine are able to stop treatment after their symptoms have been brought under control. Treatment is able to be stopped because the medicine used was helping to restore the body's damaged functions, not just substitute for them. These patients then gladly use the principles of Chinese medicine throughout their lives to maintain health, only visiting an acupuncturist or herbalist to take care of any health problems that appear as a natural result of aging.

To a doctor of Chinese medicine, side effects are a sign of improper treatment, either due to faulty diagnosis, or inappropriate treatment methods. A properly constructed herbal formula will exactly match the patient's internal patterns and will not cause any other kind of imbalance. What is weak will be strengthened, what is too strong will be reigned in, leaving no room for other

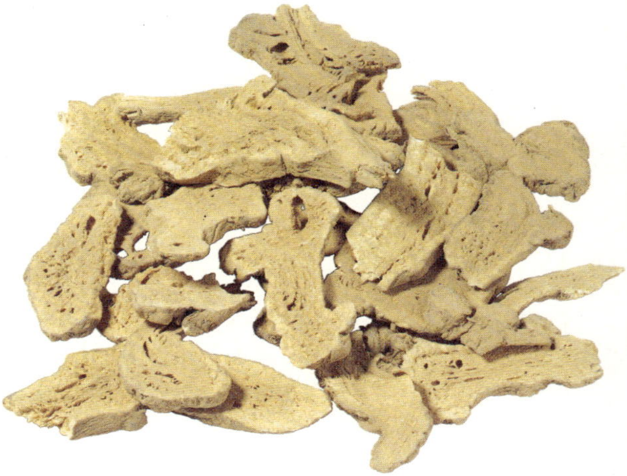

Atractylodes

problems to develop due to the ingredients of the prescription. It is commonly thought that because Chinese medicinals include the whole biological substance (as opposed to an artificially isolated biologically active constituent), the naturally occurring ingredients that make up the harmonious living organism help to buffer the body from side effects. Here is an analogy. Taking vitamin pills can help to quickly supplement nutrients you need. Yet they cannot replace food (a mixture of necessary nutrients and "unnecessary" substances) for the long-term maintenance of health. So is the case with synthesized drugs. Many of them are extracted from natural plants. They are effective and helpful. But they cannot replace natural herbs (a mixture of effective ingredients and "ineffective" ingredients) for the long-term management of diseases and the maintenance of health.

Another mechanism that makes Chinese medicinals safe is that they are counterbalanced within the formula. As an example, medicinals that take out excess heat from the body are considered cold, and can damage the digestive system. Therefore, in many formulas that manage excess heat, a couple of medicinals that promote and strengthen digestion may be added. If the patient has weak digestion to begin with, even more ingredients are reserved for that purpose. This kind of treatment is much more than simply anti-symptomatic. Each prescription must be a balanced entity, which perfectly compliments the patient's condition. When used properly, Chinese medicinals are safe and effective. This takes experience and active involvement by the practitioner. Sound and individualized diagnosis is made based on the patient's present condition to ensure efficacy and safety.

Classification of Medicinals

Every herb is classified as having a temperature (warm, cool, or neutral), one or more tastes (sour, bitter, sweet, acrid, salty), and various functions. Proper selection of medicinals is the key to avoiding side-effects. As they say, "One man's meat is another's poison."

The properties of a medicinal are generally deduced from how it affects the body. For example, coptis is defined as cold since it tastes bitter and it relieves heat syndromes with symptoms like thirst, mouth ulcers, constipation, and a yellowish tongue coating, all of which taken together indicate excessive heat.

The selection of the medicinal is made according to the pattern identified. If the patient presents with heat signs like red, inflamed lesions, irritability, or a rapid pulse, medicinals that can clear heat will be added. If signs of yin deficiency are obvious such as emaciation, feeling hot in the afternoon, night sweats, irritability, a fine pulse, and a thin

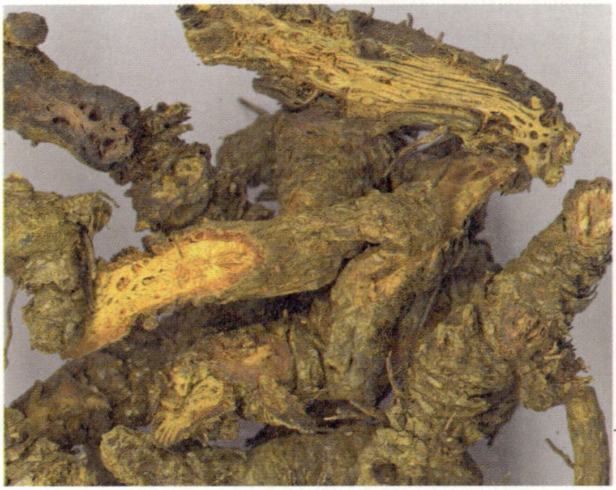

Coptis

tongue with little coating, medicals that supplement yin will be administered. In clinical practice, practitioners of Chinese medicine gradually form a number of basic prescriptions (usually called formulas in Chinese medicine) that fit the common patterns seen in each disease. These formulas will be modified according to each specific case.

Chinese Medicinals in Common Use

Chinese medicinals are very rarely used alone. But in order to construct a proper formula, the practitioner must be familiar with the properties of each individual herb. Since patients may present in any possible combination of patterns, any one of the thousands of medicinal substances may show up in a patient's formula. But as we have seen, there are a few main patterns that typically present in a patient with herpes zoster. And for each of these main patterns, there are certain medicinals that are most effective and therefore most commonly used. In addition, due to scientific research, some herbs are known to be more effective in the management of herpes zoster. Below are some brief descriptions of some of the most commonly used medicinals in the treatment of herpes zoster:

Lóng dǎn cǎo (Radix et Rhizoma Gentianae)

<Source> Gentian root and rhizome

<Property> bitter, cold

Lóng dǎn cǎo literally means "grass of the dragon's gallbladder". In Chinese culture it is said that courage comes from one's gallbladder, thus implying this herb has an effect as fierce as a dragon. Bitter can dry dampness and cold can clear heat. In addition, this herb enters the liver, gallbladder, and bladder channels, which are all related to the common distribution zones of herpes zoster on the chest, back, and abdomen. Without a doubt, it is the most commonly used herb in the management of herpes zoster, especially when there is excess heat.

<Pharmacology studies>

Modern research reveals that it can control a variety of bacteria, diminish inflammation, calm the mind, relax muscles, promote digestion and benefit the gallbladder.

Zhī Zǐ (Fructus Gardeniae)

<*Source*> Gardenia fruit

<*Property*> bitter, cold

Fruits have a heavy nature that leads their effects to lower parts of the body. Gardenia is so powerful in clearing heat that it drains fire from the chest all the way to the bladder. It can also remove toxins and drain dampness in the lower parts of the body.

<*Pharmacology studies*>

As revealed by modern studies, gardenia can promote bile secretion, restrain bacteria, relieve fever, stop pain, calm the mind, lower blood pressure, and stop bleeding.

Huáng qín (Radix Scutellariae)

<*Source*> Scutellaria root

<*Property*> bitter, cold

Scutellaria dries dampness, clears heat, purges fire, removes toxins, cools blood and stops bleeding. It is especially useful in managing manifestations of dampness and heat in the upper parts of the body. Therefore, it is often used when herpes zoster occurs in the chest, rib side, or head. Scutellaria should not be confused with the skullcap that is commonly used in Western herbalism. *Huáng* means "yellow" in Chinese and there are three famous yellow herbs that are used to clear heat from different parts of the body.

<*Pharmacology studies*>

Scutellaria has a wide spectrum of controlling bacteria and can restrain some kinds of virus. It is also able to relieve fever, lower blood pressure, promote urination, calm the mind, benefit the gallbladder, and protect the liver.

Yì yǐ rén (Semen Coicis)

<Source> Coix seed

<Property> sweet, bland, slightly cold

A form of barely, coix has a simple taste and is commonly used as food in many parts of the world. It is a mild acting herb that is specially suited for herpes zoster due to its ability to simultaneously strengthen the spleen, drain dampness, and mildly cool heat. Many practitioners encourage patients to include this herb in their everyday diet in order to prevent disease.

<Pharmacology studies>

Yì yǐ rén can prevent muscle cramps, lower blood calcium and blood sugar levels, relieve fever, stop pain and calm the mind.

Chái hú (Radix Bupleuri)

<Source> Bupleurum root

<Property> bitter, acrid, slightly cold

Bupleurum removes qi stagnation and clears heat. It has an affinity to the rib cage so it is often used in cases with significant qi stagnation and heat in the liver and gallbladder channels. This herb is also able to relieve qi stagnation due to emotional constraint. It is used in many formulas that help to manage anger, irritability, and depression. It can not only manage disease, but help sick people feel more peace of mind.

<Pharmacology studies>

Bupleurum can inhibit the central nervous system, helping to relieve fever, stop pain, calm the mind and alleviate cough. Moreover, it can manage functional liver problems, promote bile secretion, repel influenza, and build up the body's constitution.

Chuān liàn zǐ (Fructus Toosendan)

<*Source*>Toosendan fruit

<*Property*> bitter, cold

Toosendan mainly enters the liver channel and can clear heat and relieve pain along its course, especially in the lower abdomen and rib side area.

<*Pharmacology studies*>

Toosendan can stimulate the smooth muscles of the intestinal canal and restrain certain bacteria. However, it does possess a slight toxicity so it is not usually used long term and its daily dose shouldn't exceed 10g.

Yán hú suǒ (Rhizoma Corydalis)

<*Source*> Corydalis rhizome

<*Property*> acid, bitter, warm

When this herb enters the body, it travels with both the qi and blood. It is perhaps the strongest substance available in Chinese medicine to manage pain. But unlike drugs that are used to mask or dull pain, Chinese medicine seeks to eliminate the cause of the pain and restore free flow. As herpes zoster is a very painful disease, corydalis is selected without question. By processing with vinegar, the pain relieving function of this herb is strengthened.

<*Pharmacology studies*>

Modern research has proved that this herb has strong pain relieving, mind calming effects. It also has active ingredients that prevent gastric and duodenal ulcers.

2. What Will My Treatment Program Be Like?

Chinese medicinals are the mainstay of Chinese medicine. Although acupuncture is the best known modality here in the West, in China the great majority of patients who seek treatment from Chinese medicine get herbal formulas. Treatment with herbal medicine is thought to have a wider scope than the more commonly known acupuncture, and for most diseases it works faster. Another, more practical advantage of Chinese medicinals is the frequency of office visits. Acupuncture patients are frequently seen two or three times per week, while herbal prescriptions are usually modified once a week, with visits becoming even less frequent as the patient's condition stabilizes.

Similar to the modalities that work on the points and channels like acupuncture, moxibustion, cupping, etc., herbal medicine can be administered in many different ways. The most common method is done by taking the raw herbs, boiling them to extract their effective properties, and then drinking the resulting liquid. Chinese medicine calls this a "decoction". In general, taking Chinese medicinals as a decoction is the most potent and fastest working form of treatment available.

Since methods vary greatly from disease to disease, and styles differ between practitioners, the exact amounts of herbs, number of packets, and preparation instructions will likewise be very different. Here we are trying to give a general idea about a typical treatment. If your practitioner gives you something that falls outside the guidelines listed here, do not be concerned.

Preparation of the decoction

At the practitioner's office, you will most likely be given several packets of Chinese medicinals. Each packet will be for 1-2 days use and will probably contain from 70-120 grams of herbs. Take the time to examine the herbs in the packet. Enjoy the different colors, smells, and textures. As many Chinese medicinals are common plants found around the world, you may even find something you recognize. Being able to get to know your medicine and the ability to be involved in its preparation is one thing that never fails to endear a patient to Chinese medicine.

Electrical Decoction Pot

To cook the decoction, first put all the medicinals into a ceramic or glass pot (metal is not suitable, though better than not taking the herbs at all) and add water until it completely covers the medicinals (your practitioner may tell you an exact amount of water to add). The mixture should be brought to a boil on high heat and then reduced to a simmer. Usually the decoction needs to be boiled for 20-40 minutes depending on the ingredients of the formula. Strain the decoction, divide the liquid in two, and drink it twice a day in two equal portions, usually once with breakfast and once with dinner. Most often, one packet is one day's dosage. Sometimes you will be asked to save the dregs to be cooked again in the future. In this case, they should be stored in the refrigerator. There are some ingredients that have special cooking instructions such as cooking alone for 20-30 minutes before other ingredients are added (for especially dense materials), those that should be added at the last five minutes of cooking (for very delicate medicinals), or those that should be added last to the strained decoction (for materials in powder, gel, or liquid form).

Medicinals have been prepared in this way for thousands of years and is not simply a combination of herbs. During cooking, chemical reactions happen where active ingredients are released from the herbs and components from different substances act on each other. Clinical experience has proven that decoctions are safe and effective.

Recently, some clinics offer a decoction cooking service. The decoction will be made by a machine and sealed in plastic bags to store in the refrigerator.

No matter if you or the clinic prepares the herbs, when you drink your decoction it should be warm. Only in special cases is room temperature acceptable.

Treatment course

When you go to the clinic for the first time, the practitioner will usually give a prescription for 3-7 days. Each day's dose should be divided into two equal parts, usually taken in the morning and evening. You will need to come back to the clinic about once a week for the practitioner to modify the prescription. After a while, you and your practitioner will reevaluate your condition and your treatment strategy may change, allowing for gradually smaller amounts of medicinals, and more infrequent office visits. A treatment course depends on the severity of the case.

You are advised to take the decoction about one hour before meals. If the decoction irritates your stomach, take it after meals. The timing may vary with the specific prescription, but generally speaking, it is common to take the decoction once in the morning before breakfast and once at night before going to bed. Warm up the liquid before you drink it.

Pueraria

At first you may find the making of your decoction troublesome, and/or have a strong dislike of the unfamiliar taste. This is a common problem, especially in the West where we are accustomed to our medicine being easy to take and either tasteless or sugar coated. We can only ask that you recall the millions of people who have benefited from this method and give a fair trial to the decoction method. In fact, it is the experience of many doctors and patients that if the prescription properly fits the imbalance, the initially unfamiliar or unpleasant taste will become something the patient enjoys and looks forward to.

Formulas for the most commonly seen patterns in herpes zoster

A typical formula consists of between 5 to 15 ingredients with each ingredient usually dosed between 6 and 15 grams. The ingredients in the formula are arranged according to a hierarchy. The chief ingredient represents the main therapeutic effect and will often have the largest dose. The assistants and deputies either support the chief, address another aspect of the imbalance, or perform a checking action against some other ingredient that may be too harsh in some way. The last soldier, the courier, serves to guide the formula to a certain body part, organ, or channel, or acts to harmonize the formula. See if you can recognize some of the single herbs mentioned above in the formulas below.

Lóng Dǎn Xiè Gān Tāng (Gentian Liver-Draining Decoction)

Chinese	Pinyin	Dose	Latin
龙胆草	*lóng dǎn cǎo*	6g	Radix et Rhizoma Gentianae
黄芩	*huáng qín*	9g	Radix Scutellariae
栀子	*zhī zǐ*	9g	Fructus Gardeniae
泽泻	*zé xiè*	12g	Rhizoma Alismatis
木通	*mù tōng*	6g	Caulis Akebiae
当归	*dāng guī*	3g	Radix Angelicae Sinensis
生地黄	*shēng dì huáng*	9g	Radix Rehmanniae Recens
柴胡	*chái hú*	6g	Radix Bupleuri
甘草	*gān cǎo*	6g	Radix et Rhizoma Glycyrrhizae
车前子	*chē qián zǐ*	9g	Semen Plantaginis

Alisma

Plantain

Excess fire of the liver and gallbladder

Typical manifestations: deep red skin lesions and blisters with tense walls, distributed along the flow of the liver and gallbladder channels (mainly the sides of the abdomen and ribs or groin area), burning and stabbing pain, bitter taste in mouth, dry throat, fidgeting, irritability, constipation, scanty and dark yellow urine, red tongue, yellow tongue coating, and a wiry rapid pulse.

This is a standard formula used for herpes zoster. It reduces excess heat and dampness in the liver and gallbladder channels. Since this is the most common cause of herpes zoster, this formula is often used. In the clinic, some medicinals will be taken out, and some others will be added according to each patient's specific condition. Most of the medicinals in this formula are bitter and cold and may weaken the digestion. Therefore, this formula is not usually used for a long time, or at all if the patient's digestion is already weak.

Chú Shī Wèi Lín Tāng
(Dampness Eliminating Stomach Calming Poria Five Decoction)

Chinese	Pinyin	Dose	Latin
苍术	*cāng zhú*	12g	Rhizoma Atractylodis
厚朴	*hòu pò*	9g	Cortex Magnoliae Officinalis
陈皮	*chén pí*	9g	Pericarpium Citri Reticulatae
猪苓	*zhū líng*	9g	Polyporus
泽泻	*zé xiè*	15g	Rhizoma Alismatis
茯苓	*fú líng*	9g	Poria
白术	*bái zhú*	9g	Rhizoma Atractylodis Macrocephalae
滑石	*huá shí*	15g	Talcum
防风	*fáng fēng*	9g	Radix Saposhnikoviae
山栀子	*shān zhī zǐ*	12g	Fructus Gardeniae
木通	*mù tōng*	12g	Caulis Akebiae
肉桂	*ròu guì*	5g	Cortex Cinnamomi
生甘草	*shēng gān cǎo*	6g	Radix et Rhizoma Glycyrrhizae
灯心草	*dēng xīn cǎo*	2g	Medulla Junci

Atractylodis

Magnolia

Damp heat in the spleen and stomach

Typical manifestations: pale red skin lesions with loose blister walls that easily crack and are often filled with pus, mainly on the abdomen and lower limbs, accompanied by numb or burning pain, thirst without much desire to drink, poor appetite, bloating after eating, soft stool or unsmooth bowel movements, greasy tongue coating, and a slippery and rapid pulse.

This formula is specially designed to dry dampness and strengthen the spleen. It is a balance between cold and warm ingredients. The spleen needs warmth for strength, but the heat must still be cleared. In clinic, it is always modified according to the various symptoms and signs of the patient.

Qi stagnation and blood stasis

Typical manifestations: lesions that are dark purple colored at the base or filled with blood, often most of the herpes have receded or scabbed over, stabbing pain, accompanied by listlessness, difficulty sleeping, fidgeting, dark purplish tongue, white tongue coating, and a wiry pulse.

Toosendan

This is a simple formula for all kinds of pain caused by qi stagnation and blood stasis. Typically other medicinals are added to strengthen the effect. There are only two herbs in this formula, but one can remove the heat from the qi and another can dredge blood stasis, achieving an effective balance.

Jīn Líng Zǐ Sǎn (Toosendan Powder)

Chinese	Pinyin	Dose	Latin
金铃子	*jīn líng zǐ*	30g	Fructus Toosendan
延胡索	*yán hú suǒ*	30g	Rhizoma Corydalis

Other froms of Chinese medicinals

Prepared medicines

These medicinals usually come in the form of pills or tablets, though some are given as syrups or powders. This is probably the easiest way to take Chinese medicinals as it is similar to taking a western pharmaceutical. The practitioner gives you the bottle (or bottles) of pills, tells you how many to take and how often, and when the time comes, you simply take the proper number of pills with warm water. The advantages over decoctions are obvious as you can avoid the cooking process and the strange taste. The major disadvantage may not be as obvious, but it is significant.

The reason Chinese medicine is so effective, is that treatment can be tailored to exactly match the patient's individual pattern of disharmony. With Chinese medicinals this is achieved by blending together a combination of substances that correspond to the presenting patterns. While formulas are helpful in that they serve as a guide to the treatment of the most common patterns, in almost all cases a formula will need to be modified to fit the patient exactly. The formula represented in a bottle of prepared medicine is unlikely to perfectly line up with a given patient's condition. Some parts of the patient's condition may remain unaddressed, and some parts of the formula may be inappropriate for the patient. This is why prepared medicines are usually used near the end of treatment, in order to "consolidate the treatment effect" by giving mild, long-term treatment directed at the patient's primary pattern. That being said, some practitioners combine two, three, or even more different prepared medicines to more accurately cover the patient's presentation.

Take, as an example, a patient with excess fire in the liver and gallbladder complicated by qi stagnation and blood stasis. The practitioner may choose to use the formula *Lóng Dǎn Xiè Gān Tāng* that was described above as the base formula to eliminate heat from the liver and gallbladder and modify it to also remove stagnation from the qi and blood, given as a decoction. After a while, when the patient's condition is brought under control, the practitioner might decide to have the patient take a small daily dose of the prepared version of *Lóng Dǎn Xiè Gān Tāng* to taper off treatment by continuing to concentrate on the main patterns.

As another example, a patient may present with excess fire in the liver and gallbladder complicated by qi stagnation and blood stasis. If the patient is unable to cook decoctions, the practitioner may decide to give the patient two different prepared medicines. *Lóng Dǎn Xiè Gān Wán* could be given to manage the excess heat, and *Jīn Líng Zǐ Wán* may be given as well to concentrate on qi and blood stagnation, both in pill form.

The following are three prepared medicines of plant origin for herpes zoster and have been officially approved by the Chinese FDA for commercial use in China.

Prepared Medicines for Different Types of Herpes Zoster

Product Name	Pattern
Long Dan Xie Gan Pill	Excess fire of the liver and gallbladder
Shen Ling Bai Shu Capsule	Damp heat in the spleen and stomach
Xue Fu Zhu Yu Pill	Qi stagnation and blood stasis

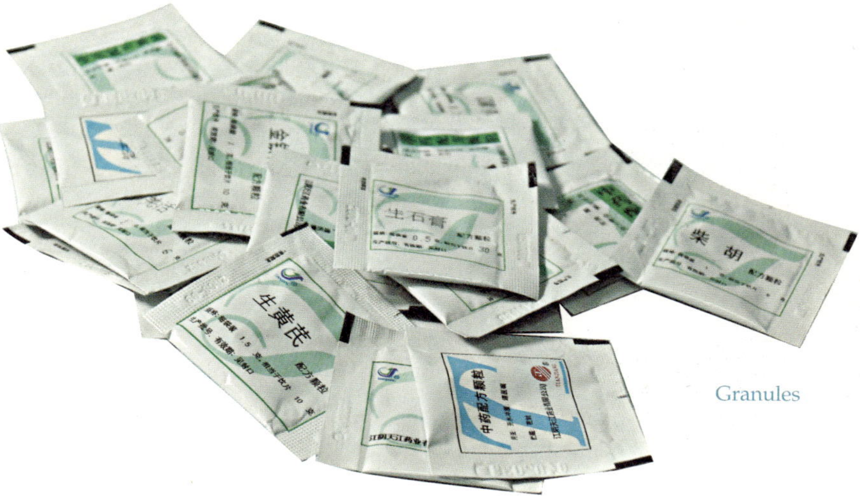

Granules

Granules

Chinese medicinals in granule form is a modern creation and represents a middle path between decoctions and prepared medicines. To make granules, individual herbs or whole formulas are boiled at a factory until a concentrated powder remains. This is then packaged and can be combined by the practitioner to fit the patient's exact pattern. The patient takes the granule packets, empties them into a cup or container, pours hot water over the mixture, stirs to dissolve, and drinks. This allows a more convenient preparation, and individualized formula design. However, it is generally thought that taking herbs in granule form is slightly less effective than decoctions. Despite this, granules have become popular with many patients and practitioners in recent years due to their ease of preparation.

External application

Chinese medicinals are sometimes prepared so that they may be applied directly to the skin to be absorbed superficially. Sometimes only a single ingredient is used, but often a formula is made with numerous ingredients. The herbs can be applied as a wash, a plaster, or applied under a gauze dressing. External applications are usually used for problems of the skin and superficial channels. They are used often in dermatology or to manage pain, numbness, and injury of a local area.

The simplest way to make an external application is to boil herbs in a similar way that you would prepare a decoction and apply the cooled liquid to the skin. External applications do not need to be as specific as decoctions that are taken internally. For this reason, many practitioners use some kind of prepared medicine, usually as an alcohol

extract, oil, cream, or sometimes a plaster that will stick to the body.

Research and clinical experience has shown that a variety of external application products are effective in managing the pain associated with herpes zoster. The ingredients used can vary greatly, depending on the patient, the doctor's training, and even the region or season. External applications are an important part of the managment of herpes zoster, and some that have been proven effective are listed below:

- *Dà Huáng Wǔ Bèi Zǐ Ointment.*

Ingredients: *dà huáng* (Radix et Rhizoma Rhei), *wǔ bèi zǐ* (Galla Chinensis), *huáng bǎi* (Cortex Phellodendri Chinensis), *máng xiāo* (Natrii Sulfas), and vaseline.

The oil is applied to the skin and wrapped with a gauze dressing. It is used to manage pain that feels burning and stabbing with fluid filled lesions[27].

- *Xióng Huáng Powder.*

Ingredients: *xióng huáng* (Realgar) 5g, *bīng piàn* (Borneolum Syntheticum) 0.5g, and alcohol 100mL.

The liquid is applied to the affected area 4 to 6 times a day. It is used for all kinds of herpes zoster[28].

- *Tè Xiào Shé Dǎn Ointment.*

Ingredients: *huáng lián* (Rhizoma Coptidis) 30g, *zǎo xiū* (Rhizoma Paridis) 50g, *xióng huáng* (Realgar) 60g, *hǔ pò* (Succinum) 90g, *míng fán* (Alumen) 90g, *wú gōng* (Scolopendra) 20g.

The formula is applied to the skin and wrapped with a gauze dressing. It is used for all kinds of herpes zoster[29].

- *Propolis Tincture.*

Ingredients: propolis 15g and 95% alcohol 100ml.

The liquid is applied to the skin and wrapped with a gauze dressing. It is used for all kinds of herpes zoster[30].

This is only a small proportion of the products and formulas for external application available. As with all treatments, a proper formula should be chosen with the help of a trained practitioner.

Attention

The information in this section is not meant to be a cookbook for you to choose from. It is presented in order to help you understand more about Chinese medicine. The selection and preparation of medicinals must be done by a trained Chinese medical practitioner.

3. Translated Research

● Xu Yi-hou et al. used Chinese medicinals to treat 44 patients with herpes zoster of the qi stagnation type. With an average of 12 days treatment, 36 cases were cured, 6 cases show an obvious effect, and 2 cases had some effect. The shortest course was 5 days and the longest was 19 days[31].

● Zhang Xiao-wei et al. clinically differentiated herpes zoster patients into three types: more heat than dampness, more dampness than heat, and qi stagantion with blood stasis. She applied modifications of different formulas accordingly to treat 60 patients. After a course of treatment, all patients were cured[32].

● Bai Jun-feng et al. used herbal decoctions to treat 46 patients with herpes zoster. The prescription was modified according to signs and symptoms. 100 percent of patients experienced significant relief[33].

● Zhang Jian-hua et al. used a modified version of *Si Ni* Powder to treat 36 patients suffering from post herpetic neuralgia. At the end of treatment, 26 cases were cured, and 10 cases had an obvious positive effect[34].

● Doctor Niu et al. applied Semen Cuscutae ointment to treat herpes zoster. 98 patients were treated using only this external therapy. As a result, all the cases had recovered within 5 days and both the skin lesion and the pain were totally resolved. Furthermore, 10 cases were cured within 2 days, making up 10.2% of the total; 45 cases within 3 days, 45.9%; and 39 cases within 4 days, 39.3%[35].

● Du Jun-bao and his staff used an herbal decoction to treat 150 patients with herpes zoster, whereas 50 patients were given conventional biomedicine and served as the control group. Of those treated with herbal medicine, 148 cases were cured and 2 had improved. Among the control group, 44 cases were cured and 6 cases improved. The herbal therapy proved slightly more effective than biomedical treatment[36].

● Tao Yun-qin et al. used an herbal formula for external application to treat 32 patients with herpes zoster. All patients were cured and in comparison to a control group, the herbal therapy was more effective and had a shorter course[37].

Tui Na (Massage)

1. What Is Tui Na?

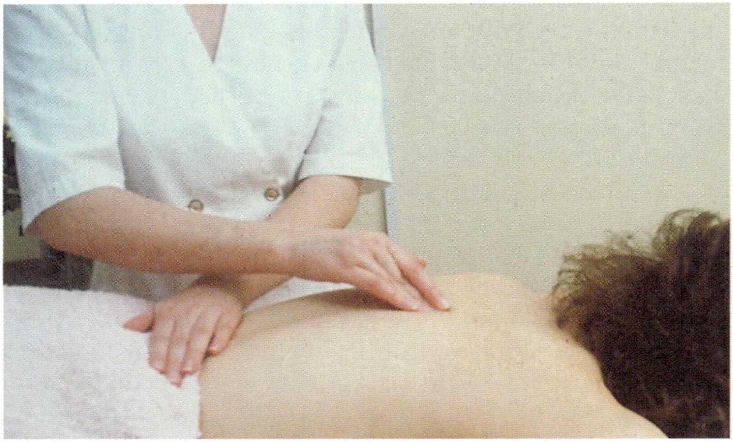

Tui na, literally "pushing and grasping", but usually simply translated as massage, is a manual practice of manipulating the body performed by highly-skilled practitioners. By stimulating the specific areas (acupuncture points or channels) with well-honed techniques, the channels can be opened and the flow of qi and blood will be promoted and regulated. The body's qi will be strengthened and so will its resistance to disease. Tui na is an important element of Chinese medicine and is popular with everyday people as it is simple, convenient, effective, and cheap.

Tui na is irreplaceable as a natural kind of physical therapy. You may have already tried other kinds of massage, but the tui na of Chinese medicine is unique because it is deeply rooted in Chinese medical theory. According to the theory of Chinese medicine, pain is either due to stagnation or deficiency, and local stagnation of the flow of qi and blood is the most common cause. Tui na can relieve this kind of pain by applying forceful, smooth, and penetrating manipulations in order to remove stagnation and promote the flow of qi and blood. Pain with a different diagnosis would be managed differently, in accordance to theory. As in all aspects of Chinese medicine, applying individualized treatment is of primary importance. Discovering the unique pattern of disharmony in each patient is vital in order to apply the correct treatment methods.

In the treatment of herpes zoster, tui na is effective, though it often plays a supplementary role. Manual stimulus on the acupuncture points (acupressure) will also produce effects similar to acupuncture according to the theory of Chinese medicine. Tui na is more convenient and also may sound safer if you are afraid of needles. If applied regularly, tui na can not only relieve your symptoms, but can make you feel relaxed and refreshed every time you leave the clinic. You will know how well tui na works once you try it.

2. What Will My Treatment Program Be Like?

After inquiring about your condition and performing a detailed examination, the practitioner will decide on a tui na procedure based on the pattern identification. Since tui na is a direct, manual therapy, treatment can take place almost anywhere and in many positions, but most often the patients will be asked to lie on their back or stomach. Sometimes the massage will be done in the sitting position. If necessary, the position may be changed during the treatment.

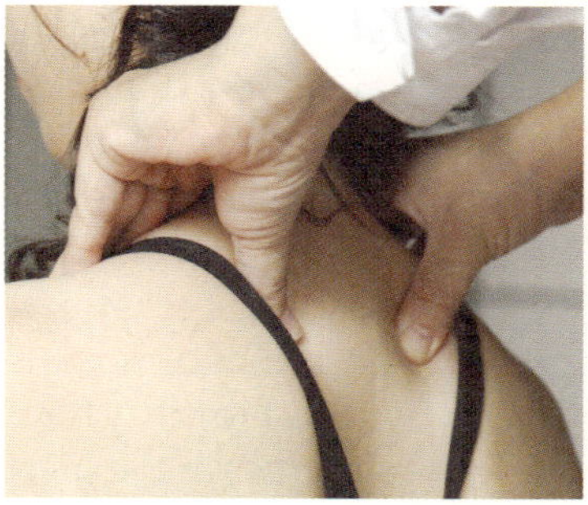

A pair of trained hands is all that is necessary for a tui na treatment to be performed. The manipulations are called "*shou fa*" (techniques of the hands) in Chinese. Other parts of the practitioner's body might also be used, such as elbows and arms. Occasionally, a practitioner might use some kind of massage tool.

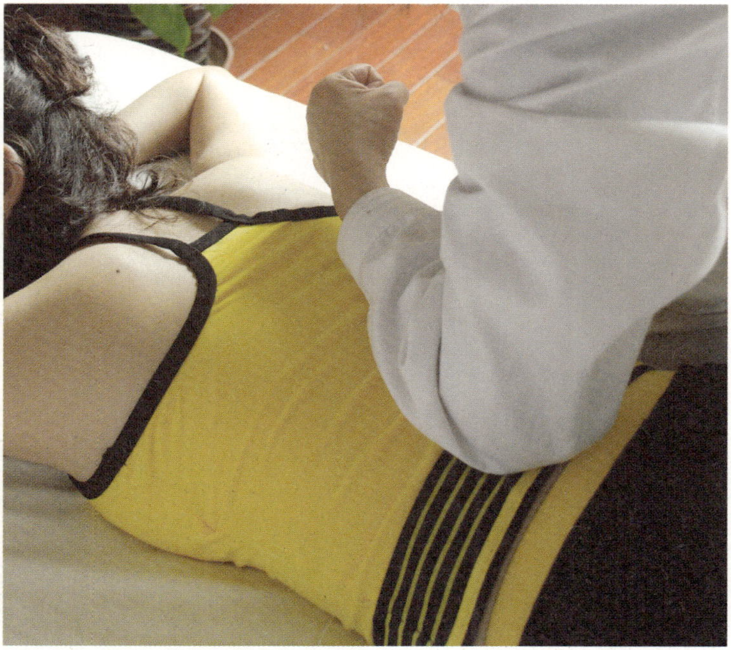

Special oil or medicinal paste may sometimes be used to lubricate and protect the skin and for their own therapeutic effects. The most common ingredients are common oily substances like lanolin or beeswax mixed with herbs that invigorate qi and blood. If you are allergic to certain substances, please inform the practitioner before treatment begins. Sometimes medicinal pastes are specially made to manage certain conditions. For example, one kind of paste for deficiency pain, another for stagnation pain; one kind for the upper body and a different type for the lower half.

3. At Home Massage

Tui na manipulation is not as simple as it looks, even though many of the procedures are simple actions performed every day such as pushing, grasping, pressing and kneading. It is actually a set of highly-skilled techniques and expert movements that are performed according to Chinese medical theory. It is targeted at the system of channels and acupuncture points throughout the body. Therefore, the manipulation must be performed by trained practitioners to promote internal self-adjustment of the channel system without harming the local tissues of the body. The effect of tui na depends more on the skill with which the manipulations are performed rather on the sheer force of the pressure. Force, even a small amount, applied improperly can be harmful to the body. Some times patients come to the clinic who have been given "tui na therapy" by a non-professional practitioner, showing bruises or other injuries. It is not suggested to perform or receive tui na treatments that you have observed in the clinic on or by your friends or family members without the presence of instructor.

Nonetheless, there are some self-massage techniques that are safe, simple, convenient and designed for patients with herpes zoster to soothe their body and mind, regulate organ function, and serve as a supplement to the medical management of herpes zoster. Please note that there are numerous tui na routines and self-massage protocols recommended for patients. The most important thing is to find something that helps you and feels good.

Simple massage routines can be done at home either alone or with the help of a friend or family member.

The first protocol can be done by a family member or friend[38]. The following procedure can be done every other day for thirty minutes each time.

(1) Use the rolling method on the bladder channel (running parallel to the spine on both sides) on the back for 10 minutes. To perform this method, use a loose fist and roll up and down the back. This area is home to an important group of points that connect to each internal organ. Massage of this area can help to harmonize the entire body.

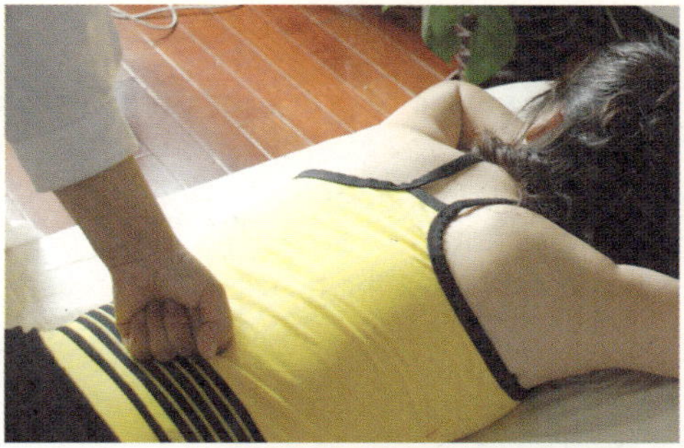

(2) First locate tender areas of the back by pressing. Then flick and pluck these points. Lastly, rub laterally on the kidney point *shèn shù* (BL 23) which lies about two fingers out from the spine roughly level to the belly button on the back. The kidney is a very important organ. Working on this point will help to strengthen this precious organ. Other tender points are where the qi and blood has become stuck. Chronic stagnation can affect the internal organs. Better to relieve that stagnation now!

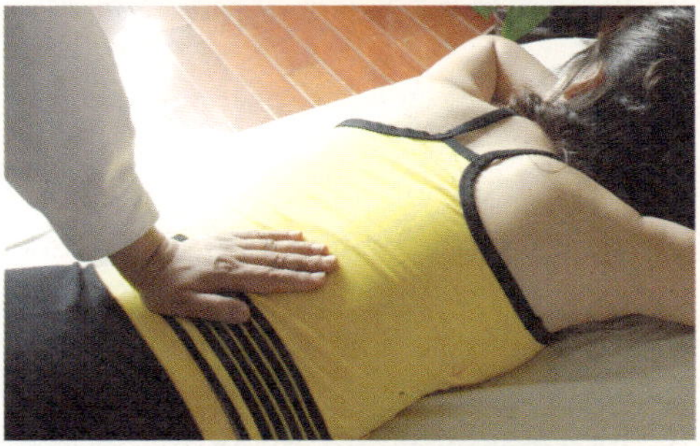

(3) Rub in a circular motion on the abdomen for 15 minutes. The abdomen is home to many important organs of digestion that are central to healthy qi. Rubbing this area will help to strengthen the body's qi.

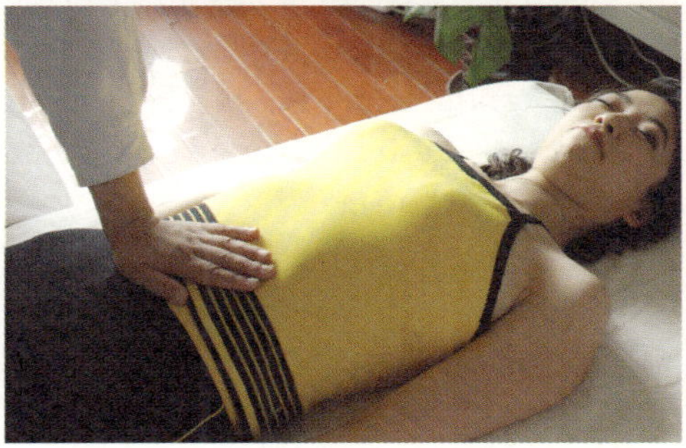

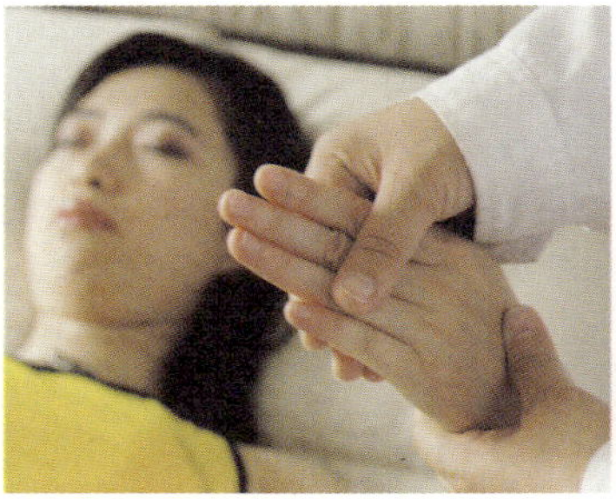

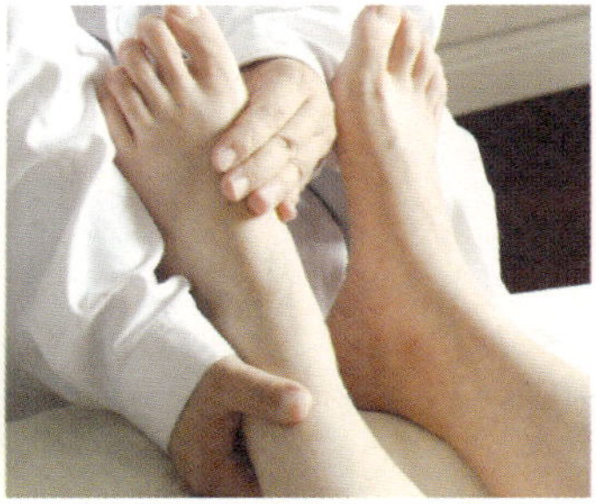

(4) Perform acupressure on the reflex points on the feet and hands for 2 minutes. Please see the pictures on page 99 for the location of the reflex points on the feet and hands.

(5) Flick and pluck the point *nèi guān* (PC 6) 12 times. *Nèi guān* (PC 6) is located on the inner forearm, about two finger-widths from the wrist, and is primarily used to relax the mind and calm the heart.

This procedure should take about 30 minutes per session.

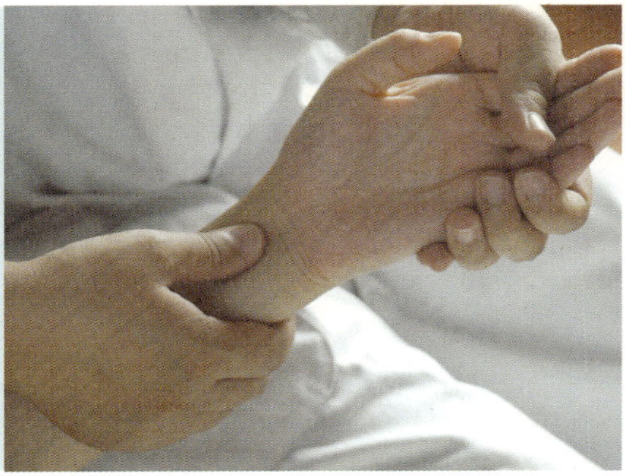

The next routine is based on the holistic view of Chinese medicine, together with channel theory and modern holographic theory. Holographic therapies on the hands and feet are commonly known as reflexology. These techniques work on the idea that the larger image (macrocosm) of the body is reflected on smaller images (microcosms) like the hands, feet, or ears. Treatment on the microcosm can be therapeutic for the larger body (macrocosm).

Basic theory of reflexology

- There are reflex points (or areas) on various holographic units in the body, such as the feet, hands, ears, etc.
- If the function of an organ in the body becomes abnormal, there will be also abnormal signs which can be detected on the corresponding reflex area.
- In turn, working on the reflex point (area) can also help to adjust the function of the related organ and the body as a whole to put it back into balance.

From the *jing luo* (channel theory) point of view, all the organs have correspondence points on the feet. There are thirty-three points below ankle on each foot. And six foot meridians originate from the feet as well.

By stimulating the reflex points on the hands, ears, or feet, the internal organs can be stimulated and regulated. So by stimulating areas in relation to herpes zoster, you will find it helpful for recovery. You can do this at home by yourself or with the help of a friend or family member.

Hand, Ear, and Foot Self-Massage

Gentle self-massage of the hands, ears, and feet can be done by people of all ages and conditions—children, adults, the elderly, the sick-anywhere and with or without lotion. Calming music may be used during the massage. Just a five to ten minute massage you help relax the mind and soothe the body.

Start off by washing your hands, face,

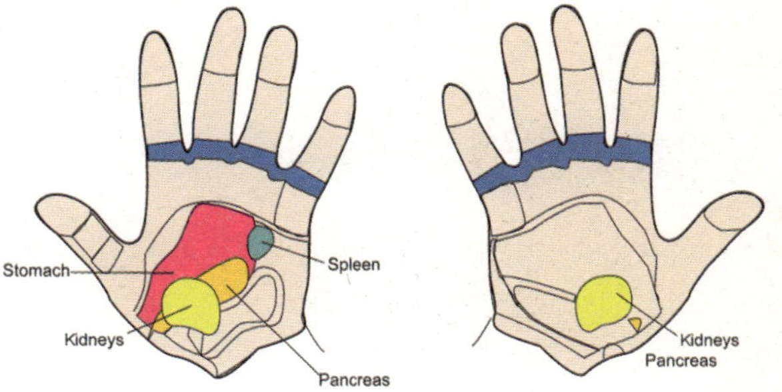

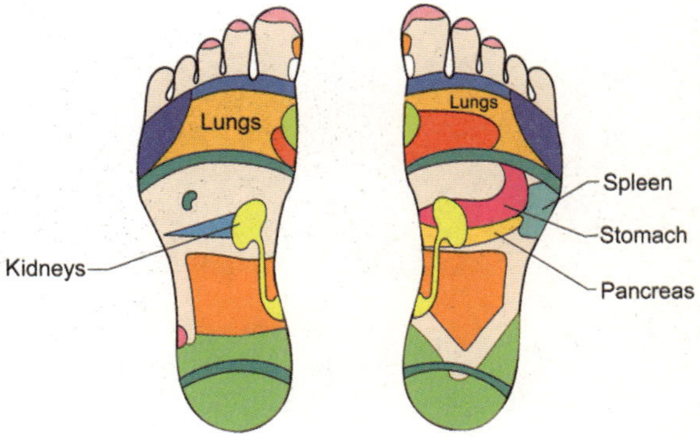

and feet with warm water. Play some light music if you like. Sit comfortably. Relax yourself and empty your mind. You can also use lotion on your hands, especially if your skin is dry.

- Rub your hands gently as if you are washing them.
- Open the palm of your hand with the other one, gently pressing the palm and stretching the muscles of the hand.
- Press the reflexology points shown on the above illustration.
- Massage the muscles and tendons between the bones of the hand.
- Use your wrist to massage the opposite palm.
- Massage each finger and pull the fingers visualizing the tension pouring out of the fingertips.
- Massage your face with your finger tips from jaw to cheeks using gentle, circular motions. Widen the circle to touch the ears.
- Massage your ears all over and warm them with your hands.
- Stretch the lobes gently and press the points shown on page 79.
- Rest for a few minutes if you are feeling tired.
- Adjust your position to make yourself comfortable. Prop one foot in your lap and let the other rest extended in front of you. Massage one foot and when finished, change position and do another.
- Put one hand on top of the foot and the other closer to your toes, then stroke smoothly from your toes to your ankles.
- Glide your hands to the sole of your foot and massage the reflexology points shown in the image.
- Massage the whole foot and pull the toes gently visualizing the tension pulling out of the tip of toes.
- Press the arch of the foot with your wrist.
- Again put one hand on top of the foot and the other closer to your toes, then stroke smoothly from your toes to your ankles[11].

You can do the above procedure every other day or twice a week. In a month you will feel better. Continue to massage yourself regularly to ensure a lasting effect.

Case Studies

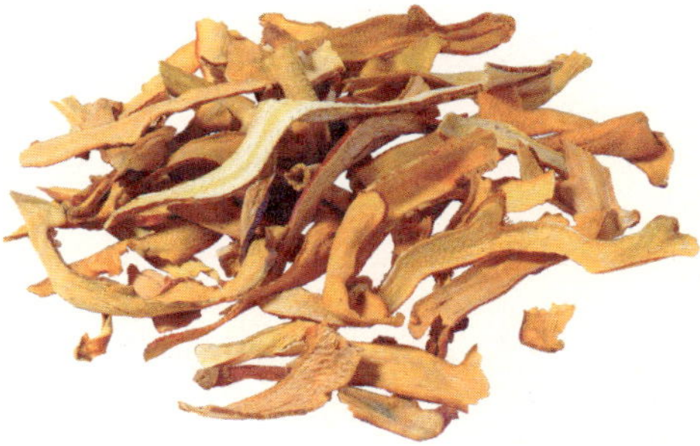

This chapter includes various case histories from real patients with herpes zoster. They represent the standard of care with Chinese medicine. These cases are to show you that real people have been able to bring their disease under control and lead healthy lives. You may notice that many of these histories involve herbal medicine, usually prescribed to be taken as a decoction. For those who were initially attracted to Chinese medicine because of what you heard about acupuncture, we encourage you to give herbal medicine a fair trial. It is the most effective, safest, and fastest way to health with Chinese medicine.

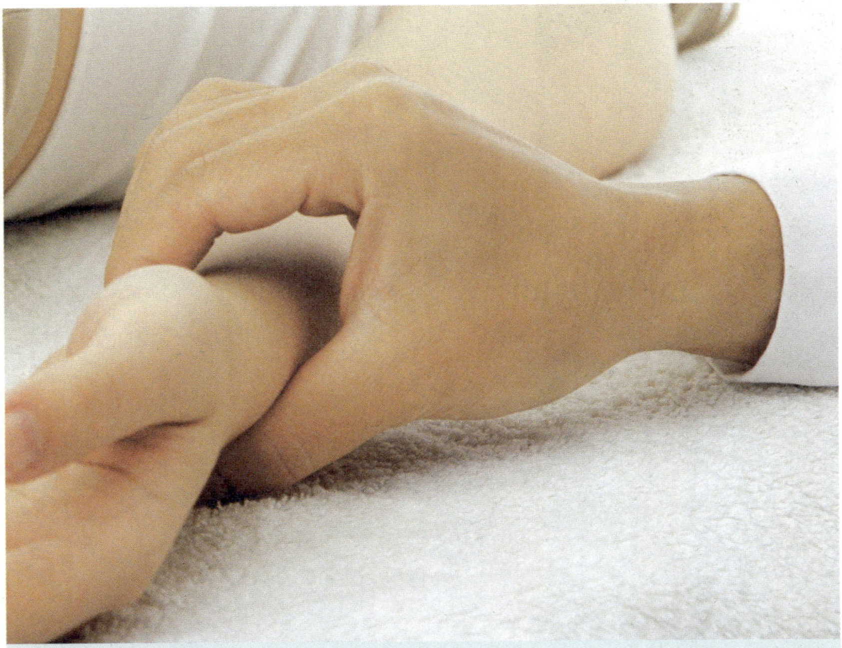

You are about to read case histories of patients with herpes zoster. All of them are seeking treatment from natural medicine. These accounts might not be totally unfamiliar, and from reading this book, you will be able to understand something about the Chinese medical theory and treatment protocols.

Case 1

Mr. Lu, age 60, paid his first visit to Dr. Zhao in late September. He complained of pain on the left side of his chest that had persisted for more than four months. In May of that year, he had suffered from an acute attack of herpes zoster. The lesions receded after a short time, but the chest pain remained. When the chest was touched, he felt pain like he was being needled, and the pain sometimes came even without touching. Though he had tried all kinds of medicine, he had experienced no relief.

At the clinic, Dr. Zhao performed a detailed inquiry and physical exam just like any biomedical doctor would. The difference was an extra tongue inspection and careful pulse examination. The diagnosis of Mr. Lu in Chinese medical terms was *chán yāo huǒ dǎn* (flaming pellets entwining the waist) due to retained pathogenic heat, stagnated qi and blood, and blocked channels and collaterals. His biomedical diagnosis was post-herpetic neuralgia.

According to the signs and symptoms, a formula was prescribed to activate blood, eliminate blood stasis, clear the channels and collaterals, and remove heat. The formula was given in the form of a decoction. In addition, he was given an herbal product to use externally.

After five days of treatment, the patient's pain had been greatly relieved and he was able to fall asleep peacefully at night. The same prescription was continued for another seven days and by then his pain had disappeared. As there was still redness and itching of the skin in the area, the decoction was stopped and his external remedy was changed. Soon after, the itch was stopped and he stopped visiting the clinic[39].

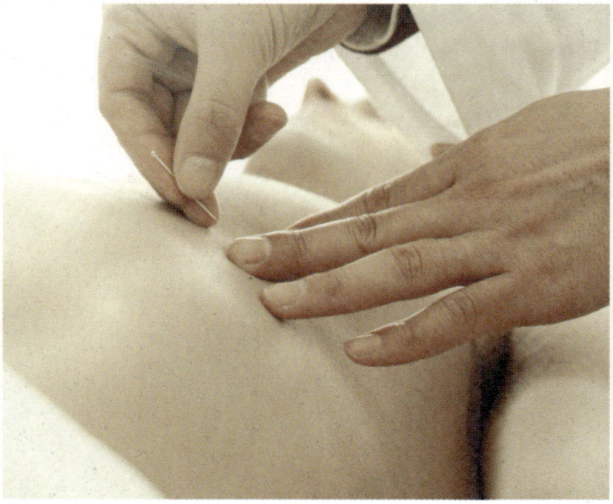

Case 2

Mr. Zhu, age 18, came to see Dr. Gu for treatment. One week ago, his left flank had started itching and he felt a stabbing pain in the area. It gradually became worse and was accompanied by fever and a general malaise. Blisters that had erupted had broken from being scratched, leading to red swelling and festering. In the examination, the Dr. Gu found the blisters were roughly pea-sized with turbid fluid inside and a reddish color at the base. They were distributed on the left ribcage and lumbar region. The skin that was not blistered was normal and the area of skin lesions was shaped like a belt. Other signs and symptoms present were a thin yellowish and greasy tongue coating, a red tongue tip, and a thin and rapid pulse. Mr. Zhu was diagnosed with dampness and heat in the liver and gallbladder channels. A modification of *Lóng Dǎn Xiè Gān Tāng* was prescribed in decoction form and *Qing Dai* Ointment for external application.

Four days later, most of his herpes were scabbed and his fever had receded. He only had slight nasal obstruction, a sore throat, and a soggy pulse. The formula was modified accordingly.

After taking 7 packets of the modified formula, he was cured[40].

Case 3

Mr. Yang, age 60, visited Dr. Zhu in January having been diagnosed by a biomedical doctor with herpes zoster affecting the area near his right eyelid. He had been experiencing pain in the area for the past three days. The area was reddish, swollen and painful, and there were tears and yellow discharge from his right eye.The doctor was worried about the infection permanently affecting his vision. He also had a migraine headache on the right side, was fidgety, constipated, and thirsty with a desire for cold drinks. There was a cluster of painful red herpes lesions on the right side of his face in the area of the eyelid and forehead. His right eye was reddish and swollen shut. His pulse was wiry and his tongue coating was dry and yellow. He was diagnosed with excess heat and dampness in the gallbladder channel, transforming into pathogenic fire. The following formula was prescribed for oral administration and *Yu lu* Ointment was prescribed for external application.

Three days later, Mr. Yang came for his second visit. The herpes lesions had scabbed over and the swelling had dissipated. He was able to open his eyes and see normally. His tongue coating was thin and yellowish and his pulse was thin and slippery. Considering most of the heat had been purged and fluid was damaged, Dr. Zhu continued with the first formula but with slight modifications. After taking three packages of this formula, the patient recovered and stopped treatment[41].

Formula for Case Three

Chinese	Pinyin	Dose	Latin
金银花	*jīn yín huā*	9g	Flos Lonicerae Japonicae
黄连	*huáng lián*	9g	Rhizoma Coptidis
黄芩	*huáng qín*	9g	Radix Scutellariae
大青叶	*dà qīng yè*	15g	Folium Isatidis
大黄	*dà huáng*	6g	Radix et Rhizoma Rhei
丹皮	*dān pí*	9g	Cortex Moutan
赤芍	*chì sháo*	9g	Radix Paeoniae Rubra
马齿苋	*mǎ chǐ xiàn*	60g	Herba Portulacae
蒲公英	*pú gōng yīng*	15g	Herba Taraxaci
生甘草	*shēng gān cǎo*	6g	Radix et Rhizoma Glycyrrhizae

Case 4

Mr. Cai, age 84, contracted herpes zoster under the right rib cage one year ago. After treatment by both biomedicine and Chinese medicine, his skin lesions disappeared, but the pain persisted. It was burning and was not so painful during the day but was severe at night. His appetite was fine but he was not able to sleep well. The exam revealed a large swath of scabs under the right rib cage and over the abdomen. He had a thin white greasy tongue coating, dark red tongue body, and a wiry pulse. In this case the qi and blood had suffered stagnation over a long period. Where there is blockage, there will be pain. The treatment aimed to benefit qi and invigorate blood, dredge the channels and relieve pain.

After taking the prescription for two weeks his pain was significantly relieved. The prescription was modified to make it easier to digest and he continued to take herbs every day. The pain was totally relieved over the next two months[42].

Conclusion

We hope this book has given you another option when it comes to managing your health.

Chinese medicine is not a magic pill, nor is biomedicine. Each system studies the amazing human body in its own way, with its own philosophy. Biomedicine sees the human body as a machine and analyzes each part in fantastic detail. Its strength is its precision and accuracy. Eventually, the entire human body mapped out in the greatest detail. A doctor's job is to nail down the exact part that is broken down and fix it. The question for a doctor is: What is wrong? As a patient, it is difficult to understand much about the diagnosis and treatments due to the extremely technical and detailed nature of biomedicine.

Meanwhile, Chinese medicine sketches a figure that is inseparable from his complex surroundings. In Chinese medicine, a human is neither a jigsaw puzzle nor a machine, but like a tree growing in soil, a fish swimming in water, or a bird flying in the sky. When it comes to accuracy and precision, Chinese medicine may never compare to biomedicine. Its strength is seeing the big picture. A practitioner's job is to evaluate the patient's overall condition and find where the imbalances lie. As a patient, you may not have the training to evaluate your own imbalances of yin and yang, but you have the ability to understand what is wrong, and more importantly, how you can act to restore health.

In the future we think these two types of medicine will be integrated to benefit all mankind. It will take time. It will take understanding. Most of all, it will take wisdom, the wisdom to eliminate inhibition and choose freedom, the wisdom to judge by merit alone.

Get the medicine you need, no matter Eastern or Western.

Appendix

Basic Disease Information (Biomedicine)

Introduction

Herpes zoster, often known as shingles, is caused by the same virus that causes chickenpox. Normally, herpes zoster lies dormant in the nervous system. It may become active when the immune system is not functioning properly. For this reason, most people who suffer from herpes zoster are elderly, on strong medication, or have some kind of degenerative disease.

The lesions erupt along the pathway of the nerve. Normally only one side of the body is affected by the viral outbreak. A rash that leads to raised blisters erupts on the skin. If the nerve affected leads to the eye, vision may be endangered.

The infection is usually extremely painful. This acutely painful phase usually lasts several weeks. In roughly 20% of cases the patient will have persistent pain long after the blisters and inflammation disappear. This is known as post-herpetic neuralgia.

Signs and symptoms

The signs and symptoms range in severity depending on the extent of the outbreak and the state of the patient's immune system. Some problems listed occur indirectly from the inflammation caused by the disease.

- Flu-like symptoms (fever, headache, fatigue)
- Rash
- Red, sensitive, sore skin
- Blisters and sores on the skin
- Pain (may be burning or throbbing), itching and tingling

Treatment

The biomedical treatment of herpes zoster usually includes anti-viral, pain and anti-inflammatory drugs. In some cases, secondary conditions caused by herpes zoster may require surgery.

Adapted from http://www.stlukeseye.com/Conditions/HerpesZoster.asp

Statistics

- About 1 in 5 patients experience severe pain even after the initial rash has cleared.
- In the USA, there are an estimated 1 million cases each year.
- About 10 percent of adults contract herpes zoster during their lifetime, normally after age 50.
- An adult over 60 is ten times more likely to contract herpes zoster than a child under 10 years old.
- Normally the virus does not reoccur because patients develop an immunity to it.
- Newborn babies whose mothers had chickenpox within three weeks of delivery are vulnerable to herpes zoster.

Adapted from http://www. content.nhiondemand.com

Additional Reading Material

Chinese Medicine

- Xu Yi-bing. *An Illustrated Guide to Chinese Medicine*. People's Medical Publishing House, 2007.
- Paul Pritchford. *Healing With Whole Foods: Asian Traditions and Modern Nutrition*. North Atlantic Books, 2003.
- Harriet Beinfield, Efrem Korngold. *Between Heaven and Earth*. Random House, 1991
- Tom Williams. *Complete Illustrated Guide to Chinese Medicine*. Barnes & Noble INC, 1996.
- http://www.acupuncture.com/education/tcmbasics/index.htm
- http://www.acupuncturetoday.com/abc/
- http://www.healthy.net/
- http://nccam.nih.gov/health/
- http://www.tcmstudent.com/
- http://www.nlm.nih.gov/hmd/chinese/chinesehome.htm/
- http://qi-journal.com/
- http://www.chineseherbacademy.org/
- http://www.bluepoppy.com/
- http://www.chinesemedicinedoc.com/

Herpes zoster

- http://www.answers.com/herpes+zoster?cat=health
- http://www.medicinenet.com/shingles/article.htm
- http://www.aafp.org/afp/20000415/2437.html
- http://www.ninds.nih.gov/disorders/shingles/shingles.htm

How to Find a Practitioner of Chinese Medicine?

Finding a practitioner of Chinese medicine is often as easy as looking in your local phone book. Most cities now have an "Acupuncture" heading in the yellow pages. Since acupuncture is the most well known modality of Chinese medicine in Western countries, those that practice Chinese herbalism will also be listed in this section. In many places, there will probably not be a practitioner who specializes in treating herpes zoster, but you may be able to find someone in the larger cities if you call around.

Most countries have established educational and licensure standards. A practitioner should be able to verify that these standards have been met.

The web can offer many ways to find a practitioner. Just searching for "acupuncture" and your town/area's name will probably locate something. The following internet resources should help you find a practitioner in your local area:

International Acupuncture Referral:
http://www.acufinder.com
http://www.gancao.net

Australia
Australian Acupuncture and Chinese Medicine Association
http://www.acupuncture.org.au/

Canada
Traditional Chinese Medicine Association of British Columbia
http://tcmabc.org/

Ordre des Acupuncteurs, Quebec
http://www.ordredesacupuncteurs.qc.ca/

New Zealand
New Zealand Registrar of Acupuncture
http://acupuncture.org.nz/

United Kingdom
Register of Chinese Herbal Medicine
http://www.rchm.cwww.acupuncture.org.uk/
The British Medical Acupuncture Society
http://www.medical-acupuncture.co.uk/

United States of America
National Certification Commission for Acupuncture and Oriental Medicine
http://nccaom.org/
Council of Colleges of Acupuncture and Oriental Medicine
http://www.ccaom.org/

References

1. National Institute of Health. Estimates of Funding for various Diseases, Conditions, Research Areas. *http://www.nih.gov/news/fundingresearchareas.htm*. 2007

2. Xia Wu. Combination of Internal and External Application of Chinese Medicine to Manage Herpes Zoster. *Journal of Beijing University of Traditional Chinese Medicine*. 1985, 4:15

3. Peter Sherwood. *Healing*. Australian College of Natural Medicine. 2006

4. Zhen Cheng. The Pandemic of Influenza Eighty Years Ago. *Chinese Journal of Medical History*. No.4 1998

5. Molly Billings. The Influenza Pandemic of 1918. *http://virus.stanford.edu/uda/*. 1997

6. Ted J Kapchuk. *The Web that Has No Weaver*. Contemporary books, 2000

7. Information taken from http://www.zcmf.95.cn/dx/dxb20.htm

8. Jin Qi-feng, Zhou De-ying. *Dermatology of Chinese Medicine*. China Medical Pharmaceutical Sciences and Technology Publishing House. 2000

9. Stephen Gascoigne. *The Chinese Way to Health: A Self-help Guide to Traditional Chinese Medicine*. Tuttle Publishing. 1997

10. Li Bo-jian. *Synopsis of Dermatological Patterns and Management*. People's Medical Publishing House. 2001

11. Wei Han-lin, Wang Hai-ton, Zhang Lian-gui. *Home-oriented Natural Therapies for the Disease*. China Medical Pharmaceutical Sciences and Technology Publishing House. 1999

12. Chen Da-chan. *Clinical Diagnosis and Management of Dermatological and Venereal Diseases with Chinese Medicine*. People's Medical Publishing House. 2000

13. Irwin M, Olmstead R. Augmenting Immune Responses to Varicella Zoster Virus in Older Adults: A Randomized, Controlled Trial

of Tai Chi. *Journal of the American Geriatrics Society*. 2007,55:511

14. Taylor-Piliae R, Haskell W, Stotts N, Froelicher E. Improvement in Balance, Strength, and Flexibility After 12 weeks of Tai Ji Exercise in Ethnic Chinese Adults With Cardiovascular Disease Risk Factors. *Alternative Therapy Health Medicine*. 2006 Mar-Apr;12(2): 50-8

15. Wannamethee G, Sharper A. Physical Activity and Stroke in *British Middle Aged Men. British Medical Journal*. 1992 304(6827), 597-601

16. Uusitupa M, Louheranta A, Lindstrom J, Valle T, Sundvall J, Eriksson J, Tuomilehto J. The Finnish Diabetes Prevention Study. *British Journal of Nutrition*. 2000 83(Suppl. 1), S137-S142

17. Xu Yi-hou, Wang Bao-fang, Zhang Sai-ying. *Dermatological Diagnosis and Management in Chinese Medicine*. People's Medical Publishing House. 1997

18. Wu Xu-ping. *External Management for Dermatological and Venereal Diseases*. China Medical Pharmaceutical Sciences and Technology Publishing House. 2001

19. Wang Shan-sheng. Plum-blossom Needle to Manage 192 Cases of Herpes Zoster. *Shandong Journal of Chinese Medicine*. 1989, 8 (2):24

20. Yan Li, Zhang Dun-lin. Collateral Pricking & Cupping to Manage 18 Cases of Herpes Zoster. *Tianjin Journal of Chinese Medicine*. 1988, (2):15

21. Liu Yuan-ba. Burning-rush Moxibustion to Manage 52 Cases of Herpes Zoster. *Shaanxi Journal of Traditional Chinese Medicine*. 1995, 16 (4), 173

22. Tian Mao, Zhou Yan. Plum-blossom Needle to Manage 85 Cases of Herpes Zoster. *Inner Mongolia Journal of Traditional Chinese Medicine*. 1995, 14 (1) : 33

23. Cai Rong. Moxibustion to Manage 203 Cases of Herpes Zoster. *Shanghai Journal of Traditional Chinese Medicine*. 1996 (7) 19

24. Wang Yan. Pricking & Cupping to Manage

130 Cases of Herpes Zoster. *Journal of Traditional Chinese Medicine*. 1996, 37 (5): 307

25. Huang Yu-xi, Xu Ming-hui. Clinical Analysis of Applying Fire Needle & Cupping to Manage 67 Cases of Herpes Zoster. *Journal of Traditional Chinese Medicine*. 1994, 35 (11): 667

26. Ren Xiu-lan. Plum-blossom Needle to Manage Herpes Zoster. *Journal of Traditional Chinese Medicine*. 1985, 26 (7):49

27. Qiao Chen-lin. Rhizoma and Galla Ointment for Herpes Zoster. *Journal of Traditional Chinese Medicine*. 1988: 28 (8)

28. Chen Guo-qi. Realgar Management for Herpes Zoster. *Medical Journal of Liaoning*. 1960: (11) 37

29. Jin Hong. Application of Special Herbal Ointment to Manage Herpes Zoster. *Jiangsu Journal of Traditional Chinese Medicine*. 1989: (8): 88

30. Fang Xian-min. Application of Propolis Tincture to Manage Herpes Zoster. *Guangxi Journal of Traditional Chinese Medicine*. 1985: 8 (1): 52

31. Xu Yi-hou. Clinical Observation on Managing 44 Cases of Herpes Zoster by Pattern Differentiation. *Journal of Traditional Chinese Medicine*. 1984, 25 (4): 48-49

32. Zhang Xiao-wei. Clinical Observation on Managing 60 Cases of Herpes Zoster by Pattern Differentiation. *Beijing Journal of Traditional Chinese Medicine*. 1995, (4) 45

33. Bai Jun-feng. Manage 46 Cases of Herpes Zoster by Jiedu Huanji Decoction. *Yunnan Journal*

of Traditional Chinese Medicine. 1993, (5): 8

34. Zhang Jian-hua. Manage 36 Cases of Post Herpetic Neuralgia by Modified Si Ni Powder. *Shaanxi Journal of Traditional Chinese Medicine*. 1995, 16 (4):173

35. Niu Xu-ming. Application of Semen Cuscutae Ointment to Manage 98 Cases of Herpes Zoster. *Liaoning Journal of Traditional Chinese Medicine*. 1994, 21 (1):44

36. Du Jun-bao. Clinical Observation on Managing 150 Cases of Herpes Zoster by Bing Du Jing Decoction. *Hebei Journal of Traditional Chinese Medicine*. 2001, 23 (4) 273

37. Tao Yun-qin. Observation on the Effect of Applying Earthworm Extraction to Manage Herpes Zoster. *Journal of Traditional Chinese Medicine*. 1995, 36 (7): 399

38. Zhang Jia-fu. Analysis of Tui na Managment of Type 2 Diabetes. *Chinese Journal of Clinical Rehabilitation*. 2003.1.15 no.7, volume 1

39. Beijing Hospital of Chinese Medicine. *Collection of Zhao Bing-nan's Clinical Experience*. People's Medical Publishing House, 1975

40. Gu Bo-hua. *Empirical Selection of External Medicine*. Shanghai People's Publishing House. 1977

41. Zhu Ren-kang. *Collection of Clinical Experience*. People's Medical Publishing House, 1979

42. Jue Zhen-fu. Lu De-ming's Experience on Managing Pain of Herpes Zoster. *Hubei Journal of Chinese Medicine*, 1999

Index

E

F

G

H

I

Q

R

S

T

V

W

X

Y

Z

图书在版编目（CIP）数据

中医科普系列——带状疱疹（英文）/叶晓等主编. —北京：人民卫生出版社,2008. 4
ISBN 978-7-117-09749-9

Ⅰ. 中… Ⅱ. 叶… Ⅲ. 带状疱疹-中医治疗法-英文
Ⅳ. R275. 921

中国版本图书馆 CIP 数据核字(2007)第 203891 号

中医科普系列——带状疱疹
（英文）

主　　编：叶晓　　卡尔·斯蒂姆森
出版发行：人民卫生出版社(中继线 +8610-6761-6688)
地　　址：中国北京市丰台区方庄芳群园三区 3 号楼
邮　　编：100078
网　　址：http://www.pmph.com
E-mail：pmph@pmph.com
发　　行：zzg@pmph.com.cn
购书热线：+8610-6769-1034(电话及传真)
开　　本：850×1168　1/24
版　　次：2008 年 4 月第 1 版　2008 年 4 月第 1 版第 1 次印刷
标准书号：ISBN 978-7-117-09749-9/R·9750